Light Amid Darkness:

Memoirs of Daphne Randall

Light Amid Darkness:

Memoirs of Daphne Randall

Daphne Randall

Edited by Grayson Carter

RESOURCE *Publications* · Eugene, Oregon

To Michael Randall,
whose love of Daphne continues to inspire us all.

LIGHT AMID DARKNESS
Memoirs of Daphne Randall

Copyright © 2015 Grayson Carter. All rights reserved.
Except for brief quotations in critical publications or reviews, no part of this book may be reproduced in any manner without prior written permission from the publisher. Write: Permissions, Wipf and Stock Publishers,
199 W. 8th Ave., Suite 3, Eugene, OR 97401.

Resource Publications
An Imprint of Wipf and Stock Publishers

199 W. 8th Ave., Suite 3
Eugene, OR 97401
www.wipfandstock.com
ISBN: 978-1-4982-8059-4

Manufactured in the U.S.A.

Typesetting and layout, **Ash Design** UK
Minion Pro 11.5 pt on 18 pt.

Contents

Title	Pages
Preface	vii
Preface to the 2nd Edition	ix
Chapter 1: 1850-99 Grandfather Arthur and Grandmother Emma Pope	1
Chapter 2: 1899-1907 Early Years in British Columbia	9
Chapter 3: 1907-14 Love and Marriage	21
Chapter 4: 1914-18 The First World War	29
Chapter 5: 1919-29 Postwar, Second Marriage and Births	45
Chapter 6: 1928-31 China	55
Chapter 7: 1931-4 Leamington Spa	65
Chapter 8: 1934-7 Extended time in Leamington, and School	77

Chapter 9:	1938-9 Rumours of War – and York	87
Chapter 10:	c.1939-c.45 Separation, Bedford and World War II	95
Chapter 11:	c.1939-c.45 Evacuees	105
Chapter 12:	c.1939-c.45 Bedford High School and Wartime Life	109
Chapter 13:	c.1945-c.46 Hopes Dashed	117
Chapter 14:	c.1945-51 Post-war	123
Chapter 15:	c.1950-51 Death of Father, Teaching and Marriage	135
Postlude:	The Beginnings of the Future	141
Appendix I:	A Brief History of Peachland, British Columbia	143
Appendix II:	Biographical Account of Edward Rupert Kelly, by Arthur Hamilton. Kelly	147
Appendix III:	Miscellaneous Correspondence	151
Appendix IV:	Miscellaneous Photographs	169
Appendix V:	Family Tree	175

Preface

When Daphne/Mummie/Grannie/Great-Grannie Randall (née Kelly), died in October 2009, she left two wonderful letters for the family, to be read only after her death. They have been included in the third Appendix of this document. In the second, written in 2005, there is mention of a "…family history which I wrote some years ago." This puzzled me as I was not aware that she had done so.

The chest in the sitting room contains all the letters and papers she had saved. I had not felt like going through the contents but, recently, being in need of a legal document I thought she had, I had to burrow – during the course of which I found a folder containing sixty-six typed A4 pages. They detailed both her early life and also what she had learned about her mother's growing up in Canada from the end of the nineteenth century, and how she subsequently came to England.

It is an amazing story of pioneering, sadness and fortitude, spanning two World Wars. It is clear how their strength of character was forged. When reading it, one cannot but be thankful for our lives of comparative ease, safety and plenty.

All of you have either inherited, or been influenced by, a measure of that determined spirit and been enveloped by her unfailing love: gifts that will stand you in good stead throughout your lives.

After the four weeks in hospital following my heart attacks in 2001, I was instructed to rest after lunch. Daphne 'enforced' this rule and I think it was this brush with mortality that spurred her on to write these memoirs, she using some of those uninterrupted afternoon periods to do so.

To make the memoirs into a companion 'volume' to the book of tributes and remembrances, I have added relevant photographs to the text where possible: some editing has been carried out where clarification or factual correction was necessary; chapters have been created to make reference easier; everything in italics has been added.

There are whole sections of her life after leaving college that hardly get a mention – if mentioned at all. These include her teaching experiences, her visit with Auntie Sheila to the Canadian relations, their cycling trips, buying a car, boyfriends, meeting me (!), etc. No attempt has been made to fill these gaps.

I am grateful for all the help I have had: from Rebekka, who interpreted the idiosyncratic typing of the original and retyped it, making it easy to work on. Wendy bore the brunt of my lack of computer mastery by proof reading, making layout adjustments and spending hours on the telephone to iron out the more wayward antics of my undisciplined laptop!

Finally, you are all lucky to be here at all, for my beloved wife had long previously declared that she would never marry an army officer! Having read this account I can fully understand why. Mind you, she did keep me waiting six days before saying "yes"! The rest is fifty-three years of happy history.

Charles Michael Flower Randall
Westbury, Wiltshire
January 2011

Preface to the Second Edition

Like everyone who has encountered these remarkable profiles from Daphne's early life, I felt especially moved by the experience. Having 'married into' the Randall family, and knowing relatively little about Daphne's early life, much of this came to me as new (and sometimes surprising) information. Michael's assessment of its value and uniqueness in the original Preface is insightful, for the narrative provides a striking profile of a unique twentieth century childhood and early adult life, and while we regret that some of the details of her life have been lost, we are thankful that so many have been preserved. As such, it not only documents Daphne's early life, but it also provides a valuable addition to the growing corpus of women's writings about early Canadian frontier childhood, and British wartime life.

In preparing this new edition of Daphne's memoir, I have taken the liberty of making a few minor corrections to the text, adding a number of additional photographs, and filling in some of the blank spots on the historical canvas in order to provide greater detail and context. Through an extensive investigation of historical documents, such as birth, baptismal and death certificates, census reports and immigration files (many available online), it has been possible to correct a number of minor errors in the original – and often very complex – narrative account that Daphne prepared, presumably in many cases from memory. In this process, a number of individuals have provided much-needed (and greatly appreciated) assistance. Most especially, Michael Randall faithfully brought the original manuscript to print, furnished it with helpful and important context and commentary, and selected and arranged a number of relevant photographs. Dr. Paul Brazier graciously laboured to create the typeset version of this manuscript in preparation for publication. Words cannot express the debt I own him for his patience and extensive labours on behalf of this project. Catherine and Katie Carter read various drafts of the manuscript, successfully pointing out both factual and typographical errors and making numerous suggestions for its improvement. Mr. Don Wilson of the Peachland Historical Society in the Okanagan Valley was most helpful in piecing together some of the more obscure components of Daphne's family's history after their arrival in British Columbia. I am truly grateful for his assistance at a number of points where my own investigations had led either to incorrect conclusions or failed to turn up anything at all. Thanks must also be expressed to the Peachland Historical Society for granting permission to publish a number of its historical photographs of the area, as well as a chapter from *Peachland Memories* on the early history of the Okanagan Valley. I would also like to thank Mrs. Joanna Friel of the Chislehurst Society, in Kent, who was invaluable in providing details of the Birkett family. Daphne's sister, Shelia Stevens (née Kelly), offered valuable perspective to the second edition at several points. Finally, Daphne's cousin, Apphia Willett (née Kelly), graciously furnished numerous family photographs and historical documents that have added greatly to the quality of my investigation, especially through providing me with a copy of the Kelly family history written by her father, Lieut. Colonel Arthur Hamilton Kelly, to which she also contributed extensively.

Several appendices have been added to this edition which will hopefully provide even greater context and colour to the narrative. Appendix I contains a brief history of Peachland, British Columbia, where Daphne's grandfather and uncle, Arthur and Octavius Pope, settled in 1898; Appendix II provides a brief history of the life and military career of Daphne's father, Edward Rupert Kelly, written by Arthur Kelly. Appendix III contains miscellaneous letters, articles and images which should prove helpful to those interested in Daphne's life. Appendix IV contains miscellaneous photos of Daphne and her family. All footnotes and captions to photographs are original to this new edition, except those designated '(CMFR)' which were produced earlier by Michael Randall.

Hopefully, this new edition of Daphne's narrative will prove both interesting and helpful to its readers. Most especially, I hope that the details of this unique story will be preserved for many generations of Daphne's descendants to read and enjoy, for she was a remarkable woman whose memory – and the values she cherished in life and in death – are worthy of preservation, appreciation, and honour.

Grayson Carter
Phoenix, Arizona
Autumn 2015

Chapter One

1850-1899:
Grandfather Arthur and Grandmother Emma Pope

It is sad how memories fade; new generations soon come to realise they can no longer ask questions of the old folks, and there is no way of recalling incidents unless they are written. So, here is what I can remember, with a few dates and place names we have checked.

My mother's father, Arthur Nonus Pope, was born in Melcombe Horsey, Hilton, Dorset, in 1850,[1] the 10th (or 11th) child of George and Mary Anne (née Wilmott) Pope.[2] They were yeoman farmers in the counties of Dorset and Wiltshire.[3] When Arthur was 10 his father died in tragic circumstances,[4] and his mother and the older children carried on at the family farm, known locally as Pope's (or Manor) Farm,[5] in the village of Kingston

back to at least the mid-C16th, and, prior to that, to Deddington, Oxfordshire, where they were related to Sir Thomas Pope (c.1507-1559), courtier of Henry VIII and Mary I and founder of Trinity College, Oxford. Another prominent relation was George Pope (1809-1860), Daphne's material great-grandfather, who was a successful landowner in and around Hilton, Dorset, and, later, at Kingston Deverill, Wiltshire. According to the 1851 census, he farmed approximately 2,600 acres at Hilton, employing some 60 laborers and dairymen. The same census also revealed that his younger brother, Thomas Pope (1814-1885), lived at Manor Farm at Upper Kingcombe, Toller Porcorum, where he farmed 100 acres and employed 50 laborers. A number of other members of the Pope family also farmed (or lived) in the surrounding areas.

4 George Pope died from an accidental drowning on his farm at Kingston Deverill in 1860, aged 51, the details of which were reported at length in numerous newspapers throughout the country, including the *Salisbury and Winchester Journal* (10 November 1860), the *Wiltshire Independent* and the *Shields Daily Gazette* (15 November 1860). An account of his death has been included in Appendix III.

5 Pope's Farmhouse (and the attached flat) dates from the early C16th, though there are the remains of a doorway and windows that date from the previous century. Since September 1968, it has been a Grade II listed building. The house is mentioned in most guidebooks of the area dating back to the C19th.

---

1 We have a family tree of the Popes going back to William Pope of Higher Kingcombe, Dorset, who died in 1723 and is buried at Toller Porcorum. (CMFR)

2 George and Mary Anne Pope had 10 or (probably) 11 children: Samuel Wilmott, Julia, Harry Wilmott, James, Charles, Ellen, Philip, Septimus, Octavius, and Arthur Nonus. Close examination of this list suggest that one son was stillborn or did not survive infancy, however, no baptismal record of (or reference to) another son has been found.

3 The Popes were a large and well-established family in Dorset whose extensive presence in the county can be traced

Figure 1. Pope's Farm, Kingston Deverill, Wiltshire, in March 1990
(Approximately 10 miles from The Cedars in Westbury, Wiltshire)

Deverill, Wiltshire.[6] As the census reports indicate, each of the children took various paths in life; Samuel, the eldest, was a publican who married and then (perhaps due to ill health) retired early to Kent; Harry died, age eighteen, at Mere, Somerset; James has left few details of his life, though, in the 1861 census (age 22), he is listed as unmarried and living on the family farm; Charles married and owned Everley Farm (600 acres, employing 14 men and 2 boys) at Steepleton Preston, Dorset; Philip was apprenticed at a young age to a stationer in London; Septimus, Octavius, and Arthur all emigrated to Canada, while the two girls, Julia and Ellen, never married, and lived for much of their adult lives with their brother, Charles.[7]

See http://www.britishlistedbuildings.co.uk/en-313383-pope-s-farmhouse-and-pope-s-flat-kingsto.

6 In the late C19th, Kingston Deverill was described as a parish of 2,060 acres with a population of around 400, 90 houses, and a post office. The property was owned by a small number of landowners. The living was a rectory in the diocese of Salisbury, with a value of £308; the patron was the Marquis of Bath. See John Marius Wilson, *Imperial Gazetteer of England and Wales* (1870-2); http://history.wiltshire.gov.uk/community/getcom.php?id=128.

7 Daphne sometimes refers to one of her two great uncles who emigrated with her grandfather to Canada as 'Robert' or 'Bob', but this has led to some confusion in the text regarding which uncle to which she is referring. The baptismal records are clear that these two brothers were christened as Septimus and Octavius, respectively. Nor does 'Robert' or 'Bob' appear in any of the various English or Canadian census (or other official records) in which her uncles are listed. Consequently, this volume will identify each uncle only by their baptized name.

Chapter One ~ 1850-1899: Grandfather Arthur and Grandmother Emma Pope

Figure 2. Parish Church of St. Mary the Virgin, Kingston Deverill, Wiltshire [8]

Figure 3. Steel & Marsh, Dispensing Chemist, 6 Milsom Street, Bath, where Arthur Pope served his apprenticeship

---

8 The first record of a church in the village is found in Bishop Osmond's register of 1099, when there was a chapel dedicated to St. Andrew. Parts of the present building originated from the C14th, namely the tower and the two-bay arcade between the nave and the south chapel. The nave, south aisle and chancel were rebuilt in 1847, paid for by the Marchioness of Bath. During the rebuilding a Saxon font was discovered buried in the churchyard. This font, renovated in 1982, has now been restored for use in the church. Also of interest is the battered stone figure lying in the chancel. It is possible that it may represent a member of the Vernon family who were patrons of the church in the C13th. For many years the churches at Brixton Deverill, Monkton Deverill and Kingston Deverill were looked after by the same Incumbent.

My grandfather grew up wanting to be a doctor, but (after his father's death) the family couldn't afford the training, so he was apprenticed to a chemist in Bath.[9] (See Figure 3.) He had a variety of interests, including botany and he knew flowers by their Latin names as well as their common ones, those of Britain and later of Canada. Feeling, after several years of working as a chemist in Bath and Shaftesbury, that there might be more chances of advancement (or adventure) in Canada, he, together with Septimus and Octavius, emigrated across the pond.

The precise date of Arthur's arrival in Canada has not been identified, but it must have been in either late 1871 or 1872. Sometime after settling in Ontario, where he (along with his brothers) worked in farming, he met the Stanton family. Thomas Stanton had emigrated from England to the United States where, in 1843, he married Rachael Ann Ryland of Schuylkill, Pennsylvania.[10] In 1871, Thomas and Rachael, along with their twelve children (including their daughters Rachael and Emma), moved to Ontario, Canada. On 4 November 1873, Septimus married Rachael Stanton, and, on 17 December 1879 (some six years later), Arthur married Emma.[11] In 1881, Arthur and Emma were living (together with Octavius) and farming in Bothwell, Ontario. In either 1884 or 1885, they relocated to Melita, Manitoba, then a tiny township of mostly wooden buildings with raised sidewalks; the streets were dusty, muddy or icy according to the weather.[12] Around the same time, Septimus and Rachael moved nearby; Octavius may have moved with them, or he may have remained behind in Ontario for the time being, as no record of his presence in Manitoba has been found.

Arthur and Emma started their family in Bothwell with the birth of Charles Arthur ('Charlie') on 12 July 1881, and Gertrude Lena ('Gert') on 21 November 1882. After their arrival in Melita, Edith Lillian ('Lil') was born on 30 July 1885, Norman Allan on 28 April 1888, Vera Winifred on 4 August 1889, and Muriel Vida on 30 December 1891. Another son, born probably about 1895, died as a very young baby. When she was grown, my mother could just remember being shown her new brother. Apart from that bereavement, they were a happy family. Their home was comfortable, though I cannot remember my

---

9 Arthur was apprenticed to the chemist Steele & Marsh, located at 6 Milsom Street, Bath. He lived with the proprietor, Mr. John Hoskins Marsh (1834-1902) and his wife, children, another apprentice, and servants, above the shop. In the Spring of 2015, the premises were occupied by The Kooples, a trendy clothing shop. Milsom Street has been a prominent thoroughfare in Bath since the 1760s, when it was first laid out. Mention of it can be found in Jane Austen's *Northanger Abbey* (1818) and *Persuasion* (1818).

10 In 1860, Thomas Stanton worked as a coal shipper in Schuylkill, with a personal estate estimated at $200.

11 This account of the marriage of Septimus and Arthur to Rachael and Emma Stanton is inconsistent with Daphne's original account, in which she writes (referring to Arthur and his two brothers): 'they may have spent a while in America as in 1879 Arthur married Emma Ryland Stanton, an American from Detroit, in the church at Arva, now part of London, Ontario, on December 17. About the same time Arthur's brother married Emma's sister. Septimus had fallen in love with Emma, but when she chose Arthur he settled for being a faithful and loving brother to her as well as to Arthur'. Both of the Stanton daughters had been born in Somerset County, Pennsylvania.

12 They lived on Maple Street in Melita.

Figure 4. Milsom Street, Bath, c.1880s, much as Arthur would have known it

mother describing it to me – I wish she had!

Once, when she was a small girl, Muriel was allowed to walk up the street with one of her older sisters (Gert or Lil) to buy some sweets. She slipped on the raised wooden sidewalk and, falling down, caught the bridge of her nose on the hook that was used for keeping the shop door open in hot weather. The sister, seeing the hook caught in the skin of Muriel's nose, left her there and ran back to the chemist's where their father was working and called for him to help. Together, they freed poor little Muriel and were glad to find that the injury was not serious. My mother often talked about the sweet shop as it was kept by a very small, old woman with what appeared (to small children at any rate) to be a very ugly face. This old lady took a great liking to my mother and always asked for a kiss. One day, my mother's tact and self-control failed her and she cried out as her sister lifted her up, 'But I don't want to kiss your funny face'. Her sister retired in confusion and it was explained to Muriel that people's feelings must not be hurt.

They must have lived in a fair-sized house

(or it had a useful attic or possibly clean barns for playing in), as my mother can remember being taught to swing on a trapeze that her brothers had fixed up, and being made to wear what she described as a pair of black tights when they played at circuses!

This comfortable life was to come to an end all too soon, however: specifically, on 9th October 1898. Every Sunday, the family walked to church. Sometimes, there were irises on the windowsill of the church at the end of the pew where they sat. For the rest of her life, my mother felt ill if she smelled iris for, part way through the service, Emma whispered to Arthur that the headache she had had all morning was worse and she was going to take Muriel and leave church before the sermon and walk home. So, the two came out and when they reached home, Emma said she would lie on her bed for a while and Muriel could play quietly in the bedroom. Then, or possibly a little later, she reached for a glass of water on her dressing table and knocked it off. Muriel thought she was bending down to pick it up as she fell on the floor and, to Muriel's amazement, didn't get up.

While amazement turned to fright, she heard the family come into the house and called out to her father. He came running, followed by the other children. He and Charlie picked her up and laid her on the bed and one was sent to fetch the doctor. But Arthur knew that his beloved wife was already dead. The doctor confirmed that it was caused by a blood clot pressing on the brain.

So, Gert became mother to the children while she was still only 16. It was the custom in those days for children to wear black for a year after the death of a parent. So, with the help of friends, the four girls had black dresses made, and Muriel remembered for the rest of her life how those black dresses were handed on down the family to her during the following years when they had no money to spare to replace them with more cheering materials. After a year, they wore black with white spots for 'semi-mourning'.[13] Eventually, the dresses were made into aprons. It seems incredible that a truly Christian family could have inflicted such dreariness on themselves, but they did! Arthur continued to work as a chemist, but his grief was overpowering. All his life he was a gentle, kind soul, as you can see in his photographs.

Despite his loving children and the rest of his family and friends, Arthur took to going down the street in the evenings (and probably lunchtimes too), to what would be called the liquor store, or (as we say) the pub. My mother remembers hearing, when she was in bed and meant to be asleep, her two brothers helping their father into the house and getting him to his room with the least possible noise. His doctor, who was also his friend, knew about the drinking and put the alternatives to him: drink and possibly kill a patient with a wrongly-filled prescription, or give up

---

13 Or, 'half-mourning', as it was sometimes called.

Figure 5. Charlie holding baby Gert
No photograph has been found of Vera at any age. (CMFR); an image of Norman appears in Chapter 2

Figure 6. Emma Ryland Stanton Pope (1859-1898)

drinking. He advised him to make a complete change in his life and start afresh somewhere else. These were the years when the west of Canada was being pioneered, and the valleys of British Columbia were being planted with the fruit trees that were to become famous all over the world. Arthur decided to go west.

Figure 7. Arthur Nonus Pope (1850-1924)

Chapter Two

1899-1907:
Early Years in British Columbia

According to the census data, after living for a time in Melita, Septimus and Rachel moved to a farm in Selkirk, Manitoba.[1] It appears, however, that they had moved back to Melita by November 1894 (or perhaps they were visiting), when Septimus died there, age 48, leaving behind a wife, six children, and (of course) his two brothers.[2] Several years later, after his beloved Emma had also died, Arthur (accompanied by Octavius) took the two boys, now about 17 and 14,[3] to Peachland,[4] in the Okanagan Valley in British Columbia, in order to buy land and build a house.[5]

The four girls went to live with their six 'double cousins' in Melita, and stayed there for one year. It was not a happy time. Their

---

1 See the 1891 Census of Canada.
2 It appears that Septimus worked in farming during his entire time in Canada, as revealed in the various census reports.
3 It seems likely that some months passed after Emma's death before Arthur went to the Okanagan, so Charlie must have been 18 and Norman, who was 7 years younger, could only have been 11. (CMFR).
4 For a brief history of Peachland, British Columbia, see Appendix I.

5 The entry for the Pope family in *Peachland Memories* (Peachland: Peachland Historical Society, 1983), 522, reads: 'Mr. & Mrs. [*sic*] Arthur Pope were here quite early and lived in the south part of town somewhere near the old St. John place, now the Campbell place. They had three daughters and one son – one daughter married Hamilton Lang, one married a man by the name of Byewater, who was a member of the war-canoe team and one, Lilian, the eldest, had the first wedding in Peachland when she married R. H. Helmer, who became the first Superintendent of the Summerland Experimental Farm. Norman Pope, also a war-canoe team member, owned land in Trepanier above Dr. Buchanan's. He enlisted early in the First World War and was killed June 4, 1916. It is not known when the Popes left Peachland. Octavius was the oldest of the Popes and Dan Cousins says he was on the crabby side. We're not sure when he came but he signed Robinson's Store ledger in 1900 and he rented a Post Office box [from] November 15, 1912 to November 15, 1919. He had a lot in Trepanier up above Albert West's and the south border of the lot was bounded by a row of Lombardy poplars. He had planted grapes, peaches and apples and had built a house. He owned 12 acres, I believe. Adjoining, or close by was a lot owned by Harry Pope [unknown] and planted to peaches with a fair-sized shack. This was often called the Norman Pope place because I think Norman often lived there [prior to his enlistment in the army] and took care of the lot. No one has told us where Harry lived, so it's possible he lived with Octavius'.

Figure 8. Peachland, Okanagan Valley, British Columbia, c.1900
(Photo Courtesy of the Peachland Historical Society)

Aunt Rachel seems to have grumbled at them and not shown much affection. To be fair to her, it cannot have been easy to take in four extra children, however good and helpful they may have been. One of their cousins was then a teenage boy,[6] and my mother told us how he would make them laugh, when his mother was cross with them, by making funny faces at them and, if the grumbles were about shortages of sugar or when the porridge was extra lumpy, he would slip a sprinkle of sugar on when the adults were not looking. During that year, they were confined to their rooms with measles for a while, and their cousin again gave them a few laughs by visiting them, though it was forbidden, and asking them to guess what was being prepared for their next meal. When they had run through all their favourite food, he would admit that it was, yet again, 'lovely, tasty, sloppy gruel'.

At last the year was over, and a letter came telling Gert to bring the other three children across Canada by train. A pre-emption had been bought, cleared and enough of the house had been built, the land broken and the farm

---

6   Probably Frederick the youngest, born in 1882.

Figure 9. 'The Vatican', Peachland, B.C., in 1974 (Note the hedge planted over 70 years before)

Figure 10. Okanagan Lake in 1974, taken in front of the house they built on the lakeside road

started for them to be together again. The train journey from Melita to the Okanagan took a week and all food needed had to be taken with them or bought from vendors on the station platforms, as nothing was supplied on the train. So, with their few clothes and a large wicker basket with a lid containing food for the journey, the four girls set off. What did they *do* during that week? What were the washing facilities, if any? I wish I knew more. I think the nearest station to the Okanagan was Sicamous, some 95 miles away! Their father met them at the station with a horse and cart and drove to their new home.[7]

The house then consisted of one large kitchen/living room and a bedroom leading from it for the four girls. There was just enough space for the four beds and a small chest of drawers; I think they hung clothes from pegs in the wall. Their father and the boys slept on truckle beds or just mattresses in the living room for some time until they built another bedroom. Uncle Octavius lived in a little shack a short distance up the valley and came every day to work and help.

They planted a lilac hedge to mark the border of their garden from the edge of the dirt track road, which was almost all that separated them from the waters of the lake. The toilet was an earth closet at the end of the back garden, and a lamp hung by the back door ready for anyone to take if they wanted to go out after dark. Muriel hated that trip in the winter. She would put off the dreaded moment as long as possible until one of her brothers (usually Norman) would say, 'Come on little one, I know what you want', and take her and the lamp safely to the closet. He would then wait in the dark, cold garden to escort her back again.

As soon as they could, the men-folk dug into the hill that rose behind the house and made an ice room for use in the hot summer months. They kept several Jersey cows for their own use and to produce milk for sale to other families. The cows all knew the children, who treated them as pets, and Muriel, being small, could be lifted onto one of them and given a ride, till she grew too big, as Vera was. They grew fruit and vegetables for sale and some were taken to the canning station further up the valley, which was a co-operative venture among the local farmers. They didn't sell as much as they should have because their father was so generous that, if anyone came to buy from him and he thought they were having a hard time, he would usually refuse payment.

Anything they did not grow themselves was hard to come by, and clothes were handed down from one girl to another; as previously noted, poor little Muriel became heartily tired of black dresses with white spots. The girls learned their dressmaking by trial and error, and it was a family calamity when Gert and Lil, making one of their first dresses, cut two right sleeves. It meant another trip to the

---

7   A branch line of the railway extended to Vernon, around 50 miles from Peachland, and this is likely where the children were met by their father.

Chapter Two ~ 1899-1907: Early Years in British Columbia

Figure 11. Peachland Post Office, Established in 1898
(Photo Courtesy of the Peachland Historical Society)

Figure 12. The Village Store, Peachland, 1890s
(Photo Courtesy of the Peachland Historical Society)

village store as well as unexpected expense.

The girls all went to the village school, though Gert and later Lil, spent at least part of their time there teaching the youngest children in what we now call the monitorial system. Soon after they started at the school, the master (there was only one) left and was replaced by a kind man who showed extra care for the motherless children. Each pupil took their own food for their midday meal and, after a couple of years when only Vera and Muriel were attending school, they shared their dinner container, using a billycan of the same sort in which at home they kept skimmed milk.

One day, they found they had picked up the wrong can before leaving home and were faced by a can of skimmed milk instead of the dinner they had thought they were about to eat. It was much too far to go home, and one of the other children told the master. On some occasions, he went down the village street to the hotel for his dinner, and this day the children's disaster was turned into a treat as he took Vera and Muriel to the hotel with him and bought them lunch, just the same as his own.

There was no doctor in the whole district for many years, and then a small elderly man appeared who was said to be a doctor, but never showed anyone any proof of his claim; judging by the extraordinary treatments he advised, he probably was no more a doctor than a man who had picked up a very little medical knowledge, which in this case proved to be useless, even dangerous. The word got round that the Popes' father knew a great deal more about healthcare and he was frequently sent for in times of accident or illness. He must have had a considerable amount of practice on Norman his younger son, who was of an adventurous nature and frequently hurt himself. Years before, he had walked up to the family's two dogs who were having a disagreement over a bone and, taking it from them to break in half, was surprised (to say the least) when they both turned on and attacked him. Although, till then, they had been the most friendly and loving dogs, they bit Norman 13 times. (I hope I/my mother remember this correctly and that it was not a lot of bites when he was 13.) Staggering into the house, Norman told the family what had happened. His father took down the gun, went out and shot the two dogs, bandaged Norman, put him to bed and then went out and buried the dogs. The boy recovered with nothing worse than a few scars and his love of animals in no way diminished.

In the Okanagan, all the children learned to ride horses. Their father had a pony called White Billy (See Figure 17.) and this photograph of him shows genuine western riding gear with chaps and long straps to the stirrups.

Eventually, the children had their own ponies too. Norman became well known for being able to break in horses, even 'difficult'

Figure 13. The Village Store, Peachland, 1974

ones. Seeing one man ill-treating a horse while trying to break it in, Norman offered to see what he could do and kept the horse at home for most of one summer, giving it a great deal of time and attention. At the end of the summer, the man (admittedly one of the local strange characters) took the horse back, sliding into Norman's hand as he went off…sixpence! It was Norman's delight to go out for long days on his horse and help the local men round up steers, bringing them in from far away and penning them in corrals. One evening, one of the men rode home with Norman and came in to tell his father that Norman had had a slight accident. Norman followed, holding the side of his face. Muriel remembered that when he took his hand away, his cheek 'fell down'! As he had been riding through a gap made in the fencing and through which the herd was being driven, a strand of barbed wire had sprung loose and whipped across Norman's face. (See Figure 19.) Skilfully, his father stitched the wound and very little scarring resulted.

In winter, the children all tobogganed and skated on the frozen Okanagan Lake. They learned to toboggan down the slope towards the lake and dig their heels into the ground and stop at the very edge of the lake. Gert, who did not often join in these childish sports, was once persuaded to take a turn, but miscalculated her braking distance and shot into the lake edge. She was very wet and the others all laughed; Gert stalked back to the house and was definitely not amused! Half a century later, my mother could remember Gert's occasional lack of humour with love and realised how difficult it must have been for a teenager to be 'mother' to such a large family. It would not have been easy to dry all the washing for seven people in the all-purpose kitchen/living room. Bath night must also have been difficult with the then common tin bath being put in front of the stove and filled with water brought in by hand and heated on the stove. Muriel had the first bath, as she was the smallest, and the others followed in age order. The men discreetly kept themselves elsewhere – maybe they had built their bedroom fairly soon after their arrival.

As they became older, riding their own ponies became the natural way of getting about for work and pleasure. One time, when Muriel was coming home from a solitary ride, she was cantering her pony along the dusty narrow road between two high banks when, round a bend, she saw in the middle of the road a rattlesnake curled up, sunning itself. With no time to turn the pony and no space to go round it, she did the only remaining thing she could think of and, with a shout and a kick, she made the pony leap right over the snake before galloping home to tell the family. This probably confirmed the family's opinion that she was as safe out with the pony as with another person. It was the same pony that accidentally gave her a nasty cut behind her ear by tossing his head when she was bending down beside it while it was feeding. A sharp projection on the bridle caught her and she ran indoors to her father, bleeding plentifully. When he had attended her, they went out to the pony, which did everything but use words to apologise!

Improvements were gradually made to the house and around outside. Eventually they built a shed for packing the fruit they grew. The lilac hedge they planted along the front flourished and was still there 70 years later; so was the house and shed, or identical replacements.

They had a treadle sewing machine and Muriel would sit at it pretending she was playing a piano. (Years, later, I think when we were in Leamington, our mother fooled us into thinking our father had come home from the Pay Corps office in Warwick early by playing the one piece she had been taught by a girl friend who had a piano. She had been dusting the piano and wondered if she could remember the piece - she had!)

In those early days, church services took place in the schoolroom – or, rather, school took place in the church with a curtain drawn across the altar. (See Figure 14.)

Most of the girls and Charlie married

Chapter Two ~ 1899-1907: Early Years in British Columbia   17

Figure 14. First Village School in Peachland, which was built in 1898. After 1908, it served as the location of St. Margaret's Anglican Church.
(Photo Courtesy of the Peachland Historical Society)

Figure 15. The Second Village School, Peachland; built in 1908, it remained in use until 1948
(Photo Courtesy of the Peachland Historical Society)

Figure 16. Auntie Lil (with Sheila Kelly) in 1953

quite young and all had two children (except Norman, the energetic, daredevil, loving brother, who was killed on the Somme three months before Harold Birkett).[8] Norman is described as 5'8" tall, with blue eyes and black hair.[9] (See Figure 19.) As the older girls left home, the younger ones cooked and did all the necessary 'chores'.

Their father was a J.P., a churchwarden, and a generally respected and loved member of the local community, and one to whom everyone turned for help — as a doctor whenever there was an emergency, for legal advice, and spiritual guidance. The clergy, who worked on a circuit, stayed with them, and Muriel remembered cooking for many tables full of visitors when she was 14 and Vera was away visiting her older sisters.

---

8 See Chapter 3.
9 Gratitude must be expressed to Mr. Don Wilson of the Peachland Historical Society, Peachland, B.C., Canada, for this information.

Figure 17. Arthur Pope on White Billy

Chapter Two ~ 1899-1907: Early Years in British Columbia

Figure 18. The Side of the Family House in Peachland in 1974

Figure 19. Norman A. Pope
(Courtesy of the Peachland Historical Society)

Figure 20. Charles Arthur Pope (Uncle Charlie), Roger Young, Winifred Heber Armstrong Pope (Auntie Win), Philip Young, Daphne Kelly and Geoffrey Young. 1953, Victoria, British Columbia (clockwise from top left)

Chapter Three

1907-1914:
Love and Marriage

One day when Muriel was 16, she rode her horse with a letter to the post office. Unknown to her, she was seen by a young Englishman who had recently come to the district and was in town that day. This was Harold Wreford Birkett. (See Figure 26.) He was then 22 or 23 years old (having been born on 16th July 1885).[1]

After leaving England, Harold worked for some years in Balikpapan, Borneo. While there, however, he had become so ill with malaria that he relocated to Canada, to farm in the Okanagan, sharing a little wooden house with another bachelor friend.[2] (I think it was after Borneo and before Canada that he did the agricultural course at Wye, Kent.)[3] Seeing Muriel on her pony, he asked a bystander who she was and was told that she was one of the Pope girls. He replied, 'Well that is the one I am going to marry'.

I think Harold was then living in Kelowna. He got to know the family in Peachland, in the house they had named 'The Vatican' (an indication of their father's sense of humour

---

1 Harold (1887-1916) was described as 6'1" tall, with dark hair and eyes. He was a member of the Anglican Church. Information courtesy of the Peachland Historical Society.

2 The 1911 census lists Harold as living in Glenmore, Kelowna, and employed as a Water Bailiff for an irrigation company. (He apparently was living with a William Constable, who worked in the same position.) Water Bailiffs were common in the orchard areas of the Okanagan at the time. He patrolled and maintained the ditches and flumes bringing water from the creeks to the orchards. When water was scarce, he also ensured that each orchardist only received his apportioned share for, as was often the case, an orchardist would steal water that belonged to his neighbours. Further thanks must be expressed to Mr. Don Wilson of the Peachland Historical Society for providing details about the role of a Water Bailiff in the Okanagan.

3 Extant records suggest that Harold had completed the course prior to his departure for Borneo. This took place at the College of St Gregory and St Martin at Wye, more commonly known as Wye College, which had been founded in 1447 initially to train priests, but re-founded in 1898 by the University of London as an agricultural college.

Figure 21. Balikpapan, Borneo, c.1910

given their surname, as they were Church of England, and given that it was one of his ancestors who, in the 1890s, paid for the reordering of the parish church at Toller Porcorum, Dorset).[4] Harold often passed by The Vatican, and would drop in for a chat with their father. He and other friends had many happy gatherings there because all the young people were full of fun, as well as it being one of the few homes in the area where there was wit and educated conversation.

On 10 April 1912, when Muriel was 20, she and Harold were married. Their marriage certificate indicates that Harold was resident of the parish of Kelowna, and Muriel a resident of the parish of Peachland; they were married by Mr. H. A. Solly, the Rector of St. Stephen's Anglican Church, Summerland.

The marriage certificate does not state the actual location of the marriage. The local priest very likely looked after several parishes at the time; the certificate is merely signed, 'H. A. Solly, Rector of Summerland'. It is possible that they were married in St. Stephen's, Summerland (built in 1910), though, much more likely, Mr. Solly travelled to Peachland where the ceremony took place at St. Margaret's.[5] (See Figure 24.)

---

4 See Chapter 5 for more information on this point.

5 In 1903, Muriel's older sister, Gert, was married to Hamilton Lang at Peachland, with the ceremony taking place at the

Chapter Three ~ 1907-1914: Love and Marriage   23

For their honeymoon, Harold and Muriel rowed round the Okanagan Lake. In the evenings, they pitched their tent and caught salmon for their supper. These salmon were so large and plentiful that they ate only the best parts for their meals and gave all the rest to the little black and white dog. I think this was Zigzag, so called because of the erratic way he ran along. They had three little dogs over the years, to keep Muriel company when Harold was out all day working, or when on occasion he had to go away for a night.

After their honeymoon, they lived for one long summer season in a large tent. It had a wooden floor, wooden walls to about shoulder height where the tent roof began to slope inwards. They only moved to a house when the winter really set in. They had 'proper' furniture in the tent. The house may have been the one where Harold papered the walls. He had not reckoned on the wooden parts expanding and contracting as much as they did, and very soon the wallpaper was stretched beyond endurance and, one after another, with noises like shots, the paper split from top to bottom!

One of the few nights Harold had to be away from home, Muriel heard the chickens making a dreadful noise and looked out of a window to see a skunk in the chicken run. Harold was a crack shot; he had shown Muriel

family home. In 1905, her sister Edith was married to Ronald Helmer, with the ceremony occurring at Kelowna. See *British Columbia Marriage Index 1872-1930*; Royal British Columbia Museum Collections.

Figure 22. Muriel Vida Pope ('Musie'), aged 16, just as Harold would have seen her

Figure 23. Muriel in 1912, the year she was married

Figure 24.
St. Margaret's Anglican Church, Peachland (c.1908)
(Photos Courtesy of the Peachland Historical Society)

Figure 25.
Marriage certificate from the marriage of Harold Birkett and Muriel Pope, 10 April 1912

how to use his gun and, I suppose, she had had a little practice. A wounded skunk will make its dreadful smell before it dies, and so she aimed carefully and got it, first shot, and hence no smell. She left the skunk for Harold to remove the next day!

About this time, Muriel had a big operation. I have never known exactly what this was for, but in those days post-operative care was very different from nowadays. When she came round after the surgery, she was told not to move unless absolutely necessary for days, and no food or drink was to be taken. She was disappointed when the nurse took away the flowers that a visitor had just brought. When she asked about them, she was told that it had been known for patients to feel so thirsty that they tried to drink the water from the flower vase. When she got home, it took a long time to regain her strength. Years after, she told us the story of the tomato soup as an example of Harold's love and care for her. He asked her what she felt she would like to eat and she asked for tomato soup, but had forgotten there was none in the kitchen cupboard. Cheerfully, Harold saddled his horse and rode to the nearest shop (I don't know where) and came back with the soup. He heated it up and Muriel sat up in bed and tried to take it but the movement of sitting made her feel so sick that she couldn't even try it. He expressed only concern for her and returned it to the kitchen. When she was better, she visited her sisters and Charlie (all of whom were now married), and she had an increasing number of nephews and nieces whom she loved deeply as she longed for children on her own. Her brother, Norman, was still living and working with her father on the farm.

My father, Edward Rupert Kelly, was one of the many friends who occasionally dropped by The Vatican, and the few facts which make sense of later events were extracted from his diaries.[6] After leaving Bedford School he matriculated, in Michaelmas 1910, at Keble College, Oxford, but left after only two terms, apparently due to lack of interest in academic study but uncertain what to do with his life.[7] In the following year he travelled to Canada: 'decided on 27th March to go and try fruit farming', he recorded. He sailed on the 26th of May, a voyage across the Atlantic which took a week. He noted that Quebec was 'all wood', and, when he had travelled across Canada, that the Sicamous train junction had a population of only 80. On 25th December, he arrived back in England – I think this was the time he was summoned by a telegram from his mother, giving no reason, so he concluded his father must have been taken ill, only to be told, after a long voyage back to England, that she thought he was wasting his time out there. On 8th March, he sailed back to Canada, noting that he was 'glad to be on my way to doing something for my living'.

Figure 26. Harold and Muriel with Zigzag soon after their marriage

---

6 Edward Rupert Kelly was born 13 September 1891 in Southsea, Hampshire, the son of Lt. Col. Thomas James Pearce Kelly (1853-1920). In 1915, having returned from Canada and not long after the commencement of World War I, he entered the armed forces as 2nd Lt. of the 9th Battalion of the Welch Regiment. He was descended from (or related to) a long line of Army officers. His older brother, James Conyngham Kelly, had received a commission in the 2nd Battalion of the Essex Regiment; his father, Thomas James Pearce Kelly, was a Lt. Colonel in the 44th of Foot; his paternal grandfather was Thomas Conyngham Kelly, KC, General in the 38th of Foot; and his paternal great-grandfather was Thomas Kelly, KC, Major-General in 26th Light Dragoons and Commander of Tilbury Fort and Gravesend in Essex from c.1816 to 1862. See Appendix II for a detailed account of Edward Kelly's military service.

7 Information supplied by Eleanor Fleetham, the Archivist and Records Manager at Keble College, Oxford.

He lived in Rutland, which was about four miles from Kelowna where he went for the Easter service. On 19th May, 'We had a picnic on our pre-emption with the Birketts. The Birketts asked us to supper afterwards'. On 14th June, 'Birkett brought us up some buns yesterday and we found out it was he who left the gooseberry tart on Sunday; exceedingly kind of them'.

We have three photographs of the summer regattas on the Okanagan Lake, some of which, I think, Harold helped organise as well as being an enthusiastic participant. Muriel had, while very young, learned to paddle canoes, including the large eight-man Indian war-canoes, and, being one of the few women who could keep up with the men, took part in several of the mixed crews.

She must have been exhausted by the end of the races. Eventually, her doctor told her to give up canoe racing or she would damage her heart.

In the photo below (See Figure 28.), the swimmer just off the diving board could be Harold, but I'm not sure. The photos came from Aunt Elsie Birkett's collection, I think, so would most likely include one of Harold.

For several summers, Muriel helped with the teas in the big clubhouse – also in the photos. I have looked very carefully at all the spectators but cannot identify any as being her. If she was on tea-duty at the time, she was probably inside and out of view.

Chapter Three ~ 1907-1914: Love and Marriage   27

Figure 27. The large canoes in which Muriel raced

Figure 28. One of the Summer Regattas: the Clubhouse

Figure 28.5.

Peachland baseball team, 1906. Normal Pope can be seen in the second row on the left, wearing his cowboy chaps and a necktie! (Photo Courtesy of the Peachland Historical Society)

Chapter Four

1914-1918:
The First World War

Before long, the joy of Muriel and Harold's early years of marriage was shattered by the outbreak of the First World War. Both Harold and his brother-in-law, Norman Pope, were quick to enlist in the Canadian army (though not in the same battalion), with Norman arriving in France before Harold.[1] To be nearer to them, and to see them when they were able to get back to England on leave, Muriel sailed to England. I haven't found the exact dates, but when they saw her off from Canada, her family and friends didn't tell her about the ship that had just been sunk in the Atlantic (the Titanic, Lusitania, or some other ship with great loss of life).[2] However, she remembered for years the many lifeboat drills and the vigilance of the crew to ensure that everyone kept their lifejackets with them at all times, tucking them under their chairs at meal times, holding them over their arms when walking anywhere and, at night, putting them on the foot of their bunk. When she arrived in England, she was met 'under the clock at Waterloo' by Harold's parents before departing for Chislehurst, in Kent, where the Birketts had lived for years. (Their home was at 3 Summerhill Villas, Chislehurst). (See Figures 30 and 31.)

---

[1] Harold Birkett enlisted in the Canadian Over-Seas Expeditionary Force on 21 June 1915. He listed his occupation as Clerk and his previous military service as the 1st Bedfords and the O.T.C. Norman Pope enlisted in the Canadian army on 29 May 1915. He listed his occupation as Rodman, with no previous military experience. Harold's younger brother, Norman Wreford Birkett (1893-1946), who was also living in Canada at the time, enlisted in the Canadian army on 23 September 1914 at Valcartier, Quebec. He listed his occupation as Civil Engineer and his previous military service as 4½ years in the G.T. C. Infantry. See *Soldiers of the First World War: 1914-1918 Database*, Library and Archives Canada, http://www.bac-lac.gc.ca/eng/discover/military-heritage/first-world-war/first-world-war-1914-1918-cef/Pages/search.aspx

[2] It must have been the Lusitania, sunk by a U-Boat in May 1915 with over 1200 lives lost, the first American liner to be attacked. The Titanic hit the iceberg in 1912. (CMFR).

The Birketts were in the woolen business and 'Grampie', Louis Birkett, had come down from up north years before to look after the business end in London. Many of the blankets were passed on to us when we came back from Malaya, and when, years later, we furnished The Cedars we were still using the original Birkett blankets, which shows what good quality they were!

When Muriel arrived in England she was welcomed into a saddened household, for Harold's younger sister, Margaret (See Figure 34.) – Norman called her 'Gert' – had recently died (in December 1914) of a brain haemorrhage at the age of 25. She had been working for the Red Cross in Chislehurst and was much loved by everyone. Her death was rather sudden and totally unexpected.

The book, *For King and Country* (2010), contains the following tribute to Margaret, together with a description of her work for the Red Cross, death, and funeral:

Figure 29. Harold Birkett in 1915 or 1916.
He was a Sergeant-Instructor in the British Columbia Regiment of the Canadian Infantry; his CO had put him up for a commission, but he was killed at the Battle of the Somme before it came through

> *There are no women on the Chislehurst Great War memorial, in respect of the Great War, although at least two, and possibly many more, ought to be there. This is not a hindsight conclusion but one written of at the time. A Chislehurst Red Cross nurse, Margaret Birkett, died at her post in the early days of the war and has long been forgotten because she has no memorial. A second woman, Marjorie Field, was working as a tram conductor when she was crushed between two trams and died from her injuries. Both women were described by the contemporary* District Times *as having 'died for their country' and both were doing work directly connected with the war effort. Although neither woman saw the horrors of the trenches or fought and died from battle injuries there are a number of men on the war memorial who died in England from illness, never having been near a battlefield, and a few who, [then] or now, would say they did not deserve to be honoured on the war memorial, but these women also deserved to be honoured in a similar fashion and perhaps it is not too late to rectify that omission.*
>
> *Margaret Janson Birkett, the sister of Harold Birkett, was a Red Cross nurse at Abbey Lodge, a large VAD hospital in Lubbock*

Chapter Four ~ 1914-1918: The First World War

*Figure 30. Skating in winter, c.1897, Chislehurst.
Harold is thought to be the boy in the centre leaning on his right leg*

*Figure 31. Summerhill Villas (on the right) with the famous Water Tower (center), Chislehurst, Kent,
1860. Number 3 Summerhill Villas (the Birkett's home) would likely have been the third house
from the near end, going down the hill*

Figure 32. Agnes 'Grannie' and Norman Birkett with Muriel

Figure 33. Louis 'Grampie' Birkett

Figure 34. Margaret Birkett

Chapter Four ~ 1914-1918: The First World War

Road [Chislehurst]. The house is still standing, recently splendidly restored. She was absorbed in Red Cross work, having taken it up in 1911, while working as a governess in Cheltenham. From the beginning she gave it her whole attention and support. As battlefield casualties began to flood into Kent, she was one of the first at her post. She began with night duty at 'Brooklyn', one of the temporary hospitals in Lubbock Road. Her knowledge of French was a great asset and she became a great favourite with all the injured soldiers. Later she moved to 'Abbey Lodge' and worked on day duty. She was working all day on Monday December 14th 1914, taken ill on the next day, and died on Wednesday the 16th, at the age of 25. It was said that she was the first Red Cross Nurse on home service to have died at her post.

The funeral took place on Friday December 18th 1914 at St Nicholas Church. The District Times claimed that all of Chislehurst was in mourning that day and, in living memory, no one had witnessed the scenes which characterised the funeral. Nurses, stretcher bearers and all her soldier patients who could walk attended the funeral service. It was the outpouring of love and affection, and sadness, at the loss of such a young woman who was held in great esteem that made it such an unusual occasion. The coffin was borne the half mile from Nurse Birkett's home, 3 Summerhill Villas, to the church, on a hand bier by the stretcher bearers of Kent 15. Summerhill Villas are just near to the site of the former water tower and still standing, although now all of the houses are divided into flats. The path through the lichgate was lined by nurses. The beautiful burial service, which was fully choral, was conducted by the Rector, Canon Dawson.[3]

In the churchyard afterwards there was a touching incident. Two Belgian soldiers in uniform stepped towards the grave and saluting lowered two wreaths which were tied with the Belgian colours. On one was the inscription:

'Hommage affecteux
a notre regrettee nurse.
Les soldats Belges'
('Loving tribute to our late nurse.
Belguim soldiers')

All the great and the good of the village attended the funeral.[4]

Muriel thus found herself trying to comfort a grief-shattered household. She joined them in the Red Cross activities, which were varied in nature. They rolled bandages which had been washed and had the blood-stained lengths cut out, made hospital pyjamas and knitted. Her mother-in-law, Grannie Birkett, knitted so fast when at home that she completed at least one pair of army socks every day, as well as fulfilling her many other duties. The organisers of the working parties found that Muriel could sew buttonholes more neatly than the others, and so she was put to finishing the hospital pyjamas and completing the buttonholes until she saw buttonholes in her sleep. As the war progressed, she also nursed the wounded in hospital. She must have found it hard work, but she put into it all the care and gentleness she longed to give Harold and her brother, Norman.

---

3 Canon James Dawson was Rector of St. Nicholas, Chislehurst, from 1902 to 1930.

4 Yvonne Auld, *For King and Country. The Men of Chislehurst who Fell in the Great War 1914-1919*, 2nd ed. (2010), 136-7.

Figure 35.
Abbey Lodge, Chislehurst, where Margaret worked for the Red Cross until taken ill in December 1914

Figure 36.
St Nicholas, Chislehurst, the site of Margaret Birkett's Funeral Service on 18 December 1914.
(It remains uncertain whether this, the principal parish church in Chislehurst, was where the Birkett family worshipped, as Harold's memorial service was held at St John's, a mission church located near their home, which was built in 1886, deconsecrated in 1933, and finally demolished in 1998)

Figure 37. Edward Rupert Kelly in 1915

Edward Kelly was now back in England and, despite his short sight, got himself into the army by learning the eye chart by heart, a ploy that the examiners were probably well aware of. When he was on leave, still stationed in England, he visited the Birketts and Muriel. (I wonder if he noticed the unheated dining room in winter. The Birketts maintained that it was better for people's digestion to eat in a cool/cold room and that it helped the war effort to economise on fuel, so the coal fire was never lit!) After a frustrating time in England, Edward went to France.[5]

The list in the national papers of wounded, killed and missing grew longer and longer as the months passed. The battle of the Somme began and Muriel's brother, Norman, died of wounds there.[6]

Three months later, there was a letter from a sergeant who had been in the same trench as Harold, and wounded when Harold was killed. The official telegram came several days later, after Grampie Birkett had visited the sergeant in hospital in England. Passing into a state of severe shock, Muriel was almost unconscious for three days and nights and all that time his mother, Agnes, nursed her and hardly left her.

The details of Harold's death are not altogether clear. The Battle of Pozières was fought between 23 July and 3 September, primarily by Australian (not Canadian) soldiers. The Battle of Mouquet Farm (a part of the larger Battle of Pozières, itself a part of the still larger Battle of the Somme), during which Harold died, began on 10 August with Australian soldiers, and continued until 26 September. On 5 September, the Canadian Corps relieved the Anzac Corps. Four days later, Harold was killed in action.[7]

The following account of the Battle of Mouquet Farm during (and around) 9 September 1916 appears in the official history of the Canadian Expeditionary Force:

> *The Australians' final attempt to capture Mouquet Farm was made on 3 September by their 13th Brigade, which had the 13th Battalion of the relieving 3rd Canadian Brigade, temporarily under command. The attack, while failing to secure the farm, gained 300 yards of Fabeck Graben, a German trench running north-eastward towards Courcelette. In attempting to extend this holding two companies of the Canadian battalion suffered 322 casualties. The relief of the Australians was completed on the morning of the 5th, and for three more days the 3rd Canadian*

---

5 As disclosed in the pages of his diary.

6 Norman died on 4 June 1916 at the age of 29 of a compound fracture of the right leg at the Number 3 Canadian Casualty Clearing Station, which was then located at Remy Siding, near Poperinghe, seven miles west of Ypres, Belgium. See *Canadian War Graves Register, 1916*; *War Diaries of the 3rd Canadian Causality Clearing Station*, June 1916, page 5, http://data2.collectionscanada.ca/e/e061/e001510615.jpg. At the time of his death, he was a private in the 7th Bn. of the British Columbia Regiment of the 1st Canadian Division, service number 442239. See http://www.lijssenthoek.be/en/address/4506/-norman-allen-pope.html; *Cariboo Observer*, 1 July 1916. Norman's obituary in the local newspaper celebrated his earlier prominence in hockey, boating and as a crew member of the Peachland war canoe. See *Kelowna Record*, 22 June 1916.

7 The *Canadian War Graves Register* states that Harold was 'killed in action' while fighting at Mouquet Farm, Courcelette. His entry in the Register of the Vimy Memorial (page 35) reads as follows: 'Son of Louis and Agnes Birkett, of 3, Summerhill, Chislehurst, Kent, England; husband of Muriel Vida Birkett (now Kelly), of 85, Fairfield Rd., Winchester, Hampshire, England'. In his will, Harold left his personal effects, valued at £137, 0s. 8d. to his wife, Muriel. See the *Index of Wills and Administration for England and Wales*, 1916.

Chapter Four ~ 1914-1918: The First World War   37

Figure 38. Operating Theatre, Number 3 Canadian Casualty Clearing Station, Remy Siding, Belgium, July 1916

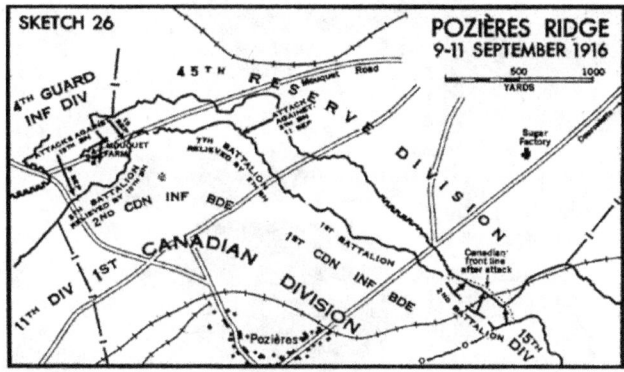

Figure 39. Map of the Battle of Mouquet Farm, 9-11 September 1916. The location of Harold's Battalion (the 7th) can be seen in the centre of the map

Figure 40. Mouquet Farm after the Battle, September 1916

SERGEANT-INSTRUCTOR H. W. BIRKETT.

We regret to have to record the death in action of Sergeant-Instructor Harold Wreford Birkett, elder son of Mr. and Mrs. Louis Birkett, Summer-hill, Chislehurst. Sergeant Birkett was born in 1885, and educated at Haileybury College and the South-Eastern Agricultural College, Wye. After two years in Borneo he went to Canada, where he remained seven years, and in 1912 married Muriel, youngest daughter of A. N. Pope, of Peachland, B.C. Enlisting in the Canadian Army, he came over to England, became a Sergeant-Instructor in bomb-throwing, musketry, &c., and proceeded to the Front in June last, where he was killed by a shell on 9th September.

The following letter has been received from the officer commanding his company:

"By now I expect you will have heard the sad news of your dear husband's death in action. No words of mine can possibly convey the deep sympathy which I and the whole of No. 4 Company feel for you, but I think you will understand.

Your husband was killed quite instantaneously by a shell during a heavy bombardment. We buried him behind the trench and marked his grave as well as possible. Your husband was a soldier and a gentleman from head to toe, and I am quite sure that he would wish to meet no other end than the one he did meet, facing the enemy. We all feel his loss very keenly, because he was so cool and cheerful under all conditions. If there is anything else I can do for you, I shall be honoured if you would let me know."

A memorial service was held at St John's, Chislehurst, on Wednesday morning, conducted by the Rev. A. Murray, and was attended by members of the family and a number of friends. Among those present was Second-Lieutenant Norman Birkett, who has been in hospital for eleven months with a bad leg wound.

Much sympathy is felt with Mr. and Mrs. Birkett, who have now lost a son and daughter through the war. Miss Margaret Janson Birkett passed away in December, 1914, her death being hastened by her great devotion to her Red Cross duties.

Figure 41. Newspaper report of Harold's death on 9th September 1916

Figure 42. Canadian Memorial at Courcelette
It commemorates those (such as Harold Birkett) who fell in battle with no known grave

Figure 43. Battlefield Graves, Pozières, 1916

Figure 44.
Harold Birkett's Name Inscribed on the First Panel of the War Memorial at Chislehurst, Kent

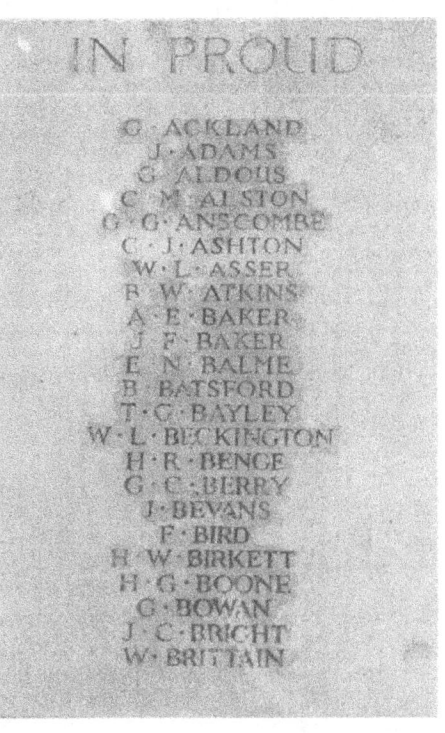

Figure 45.
St John's Mission Church, Chislehurst, site of Harold Birkett's Memorial Service

Figure 46. The War Memorial, Peachland, was moved to Cenotaph Park, 2008

Figure 47. War Memorial, Peachland, BC, in 1974. It memorializes the names of Norman Allan Pope, Daphne's uncle, and Harold Birkett, her mother's first husband, both of whom died in 1916 at the Battle of the Somme

Figure 48. Silver Cross on a Purple Ribbon Given to War Widows in WWI

Figure 49. Canadian National Vimy Memorial, Pas de Calais, France, where Harold Birkett is honoured

Brigade continued to hold under heavy fire and frequent counter-attack more than two thousand yards of line, including the captured portion of Fabeck Graben. The brigade's 970 casualties in this period gave it good reason to remember its first tour of duty at the Somme. Early on 8 September, during a relief by the 2nd Brigade, the Germans regained the now almost obliterated section of Fabeck Graben.

Next day the Canadians slightly improved their positions, when the 2nd Canadian Battalion captured a portion of a German trench about 500 yards long south of the Cambrai road. In gaining and retaining its objective (and thereby earning the congratulations of the Commander-in-Chief) the battalion owed much to the valour of one of its junior N.C.Os.—Corporal Leo Clarke. While clearing a continuation of the newly-captured trench during the construction of a permanent block on the battalion flank, most of the members of his small bombing party were killed or wounded and their supply of grenades was exhausted. Clarke was building a temporary barricade when an enemy party of twenty, led by two officers, counterattacked down the trench. Coolly the corporal fought them off. Twice he emptied into the Germans his own revolver, and then two abandoned enemy rifles. He shot and killed an officer who had bayoneted him in the leg, and he is credited with having killed or wounded at least sixteen enemy before the rest turned in flight. Then he shot down four more of the fleeing Germans, and captured a fifth-the sole enemy survivor. His courageous action brought Corporal Clarke the first of two Victoria Crosses to be won by his battalion. He was killed five weeks later, before the award was announced.[8]

The entry for Harold Birkett in *For King and Country* reads as follows:

Sergeant-Instructor Harold Wreford Birkett of the [7th Battalion, 1st Canadian Division] Canadian Infantry (British Columbia Regiment) was killed in action at Pozières on 9th September 1916, aged 31. He was born [16 July] in 1885 at Richmond Cottage, Church Row, Chislehurst. He was the elder son of Louis and Agnes Birkett. At the time of his death his parents were living at 2 [sic] Summerhill Villas, just near to 'The Ramblers Rest'. He was educated at Haileybury College and the South Eastern Agricultural College, Wye. After spending 2 years in Borneo, he went to Canada and remained there for 7 years. During that time he married Muriel Pope in 1912. In the 1911 Canadian Census Harold Birkett was working as a water bailiff on a farm....He is remembered with honour on the [Canadian National] VIMY MEMORIAL, Pas de Calais.[9]

Gradually, Muriel began to get about again and, trying to submerge her grief in work, she trained as a dental mechanic. By not taking holidays, she did a year's course in nine months, and then worked in London. She was one of the first women to qualify in this work. The part of the work she liked best was helping with the wounded soldiers. She made splints for broken jaws or loosened teeth, or worse, and the dentist would call her up from the cellar where she worked to help fit them. The patients would see her widow's medallion on its purple ribbon round her neck and the sympathy expressed in 'Where was it missis?' helped her.

8 Colonel G.W.L. Nicholson, C.D., *Canadian Expeditionary Force 1914-1919. The Official History of the Canadian Army in the First World War* (Ottawa, 1960), 166-7.

9 Auld, *For King and Country*, 61.

The rationing system in the First World War was not as well organised as in the Second, and restaurants sometimes had nothing to serve customers. I remember her telling us about the place she quite regularly went to for a meal in her very short lunch break while she was working in London. The waitress would try to keep a pudding for her, presenting her triumphantly with a small, stodgy piece of steamed pudding whenever possible, or, when not, apologizing for its absence. My mother always enjoyed it regardless of its condition.

Despite the grief-induced, ravenous hunger she sometimes suffered, she lost a lot of weight and must have been like a sparrow, as she wasn't big to start with! She commuted to the dentist's by train every day and then back by train in the evenings. One evening, there was a long wait for a train and she was so tired that she lay down on the bench and woke up quite a lot later to find a Salvation Army 'lass' sitting on the end of the bench. My mother said it was like seeing an angel smile at her and the 'lass' said, 'We have a hostel which is warmer and safer than this bench if you need a bed tonight,' but my mother explained she was on her way home and had just been overcome by weariness. The girl had been sitting there a long time to see that no one molested her while she was asleep.

Figure 50.
Lijssenthoek Military Cemetery, Belgium, where Norman Allan Pope (Daphne's Uncle) is buried (left); Memorial Plaque Presented to Norman's Next of Kin (right)

Figure 51. Norman Allen Pope, died 4 June 1916, aged 29, is buried at Lijssenthoek Military Cemetery, Belgium. The age on gravestone is incorrect, as he was born 28 April 1887 and died on 4 June 1916

Chapter Five

1919-1929:
Postwar, Second Marriage and Births

With the war rapidly winding down, Muriel decided that she should return to Canada. She departed from Southampton on the RMS Olympic (then one of the largest steamships in the world), arriving in New York City on 12 October 1918, just a month before the formal cessation of hostilities in Europe.[1] (See Figure 52.)

After visiting her father and siblings in the Okanagan Valley, Muriel settled in a flat in Vancouver, where she went to work for a dentist. Sometime later, her nephew, Arthur Lang (Gert's eldest son), came to Vancouver and lived with her for three years.[2] She had been 13 when Arthur was born; now he was going to university. Enrolling as a day (as opposed to a residential) student was less expensive, and none of the girls had married into money! So Arthur had the small second bedroom in Muriel's flat, and every evening he studied in the living room they shared. She told us how worried she felt when she saw him apparently turning pages over faster than she thought anyone could read, but he had a brilliant mind, passed all the exams with distinction, and became a geologist for the Canadian government.

---

1 Canadian Passenger List, 1865-1935. On the Canadian emigration form, Muriel stated that she intended to reside in Vernon, British Columbia, but, as Vernon was the largest town in the Okanagan Valley, it may have been listed as a formality.

2 Arthur Hamilton Lang (1905-1990), B.A., 1927, M.A. 1928, University of British Columbia; Ph.D., 1930, Princeton University, became an eminent Canadian geologist. He was de-scribed playfully in the university yearbook as "the boy with the skin you love to touch. Comes from the Okanagan, where the bloom's on the peach. He was once a science man, though you would not believe it now. Very witty. Heard [asking] in Geology lecture: 'Please, sir, how can you tell how much gas there is in a gas well?' 'Use a pilot-tube.' 'Can you use this for oil, too?' Yes, folks, he's our Equine Engineer.' See *The Totem*, University of British Columbia, 1927, 23. A memorial of his life and career has been included in Appendix III.

When Arthur graduated from university, his younger brother, Larry, came to stay with Muriel while he attended university.[3] He did well, too, but took more time to absorb the text books! Then her father came to live with her.

All this time my father, Edward Kelly, had been corresponding with Muriel and, in about 1922, he wrote and said that, though he had had many girlfriends, he had never known anyone he had come to love as much as her and would she come to England and marry him. He had been wounded twice in the war and then had the motorbike accident which gave him gangrene, following which he had his leg amputated above the knee. After much thought, and though not wanting to leave her father who was at that time in failing health, she accepted. Her father went to live in Vancouver with her sister, Vera, and her husband, Frank

Figure 52. RMS Olympic

Figure 53. Arthur Lang with Daphne in 1953

---

3 Lawrence Allen Lang (1908-1999), B.A., 1931, University of British Columbia, had a career as an insurance agent in Vancouver. He was married (in 1946) to Florence Josephine Goulding (b.1910), with whom he had two daughters, Susan and Debbie. He was described in his college yearbook in the following manner: 'Larry is the customary and more accredited termination. His perpetually happy disposition arises from a faculty of obtaining real and intense enjoyment from little things, while at the same time not allowing trifling annoyances to destroy his equilibrium. Larry is to be found in the Caf. any afternoon, discussing philosophy in the dialectical manner, and smoking the inevitable pipe. His ability to work hard when he wants to, will carry him to success in his chosen profession, education.' See *The Totem*, University of British Columbia, 1931, 37.

Figure 54. Susan, Debbie and Larry Lang, Sheila Kelly and Florence Lang in 1953

Bywater, and their girls, Joan and Phyllis (whose second name is Muriel). I think it was actually while she was coming over to England that her father died during May 1924.[4]

Muriel's in-laws, the Birketts, had all expressed their happiness that she was going to marry Edward, and welcomed her back to England and into their family as a returning daughter. The Birketts gave her the wedding and reception. The wedding cake, when made, was put in the front window of the Chislehurst house for local passersby to see. (Was this common practice, I wonder?) The eldest daughter, Mary, now married to the Revd William P. Parker, a clergyman based in Calais and looking after the Anglican church and community there, used to supplement their small income by bringing the latest French fashions back to Chislehurst and having the equivalent of modern 'Tupperware parties' for friends and neighbours. She gave Muriel the dresses for her wedding and 'going away'. Our mother told us, years later, 'and never tell kind Auntie Mary I have told you,' that she felt they were rather too fashionable for her and she might have preferred clothes she could have

---

4   Muriel arrived in Liverpool on 17 May 1924 aboard the SS Montcalm of the Canadian Pacific Line. See UK Incoming Passenger List, 1868-1960. Her father, Arthur, died on 10 May 1924.

worn more afterwards. So they were married on 19th July 1924.[5]

My father's elder brother, Conyngham, was very ill at the time and died a few days later, so my parents were recalled from their honeymoon to Bedford for the funeral.[6]

I should have included more about my father and his family but I don't know as much because it was my mother who told us more bedtime stories! Quite a lot of dates and information can be extracted from the photos and memoirs that my cousin, Apphia Willett (née Kelly), kindly photocopied for me some years ago, and from Michael Bulkley, son of our father's sister, Kathleen, who did the same. (I have found some mistakes in Michael Bulkley's writings, and his researches do tend to concentrate on any relatives and ancestors with rank or title. He didn't even get Harold's name right in his very brief footnote; one of those few who maybe think that living in a wooden house and pioneering farming makes one any less truly 'gentlefolk'. He might have thought differently if he had taken the trouble to find out that Muriel's ancestors were landowners and yeoman in the West Country, and finally put themselves in a very difficult position financially when they built the church of St Andrew and St Peter in the village of Toller Porcorum, or 'Great Toller', in Dorset.)[7] (See Figure 57.)

Figure 55. Top: Edward and Muriel on their wedding day

Figure 56. Below: Muriel in her 'going away' hat!

---

5 The same date as Daphne and Michael Randall's marriage in 1956, though I did not know it until I read these memoirs! It was also my birthday, as well as the day I became eligible for the Army Marriage Allowance! Coincidently my father also married on his birthday. (CMFR)

6 James Conyngham Kelly died, age 35, on 25 July 1924 in London.

7 This well-known and much admired parish church is actually medieval, though the south aisle was added in 1891; three years later, the gallery and box pews were removed. It is, presumably, this reorder-

Chapter Five ~ 1919-1929: Postwar, Second Marriage and Births

Figure 57. Church of St Andrew and St Peter, Toller Porcorum (or 'Great Toller'), Dorset (the south aisle is in the foreground on the left)

There is one thing I do remember our father telling us when we asked him for a bedtime story about when he was little. This pertained to the first – and only – time he decided not to go back to Bedford School for afternoon lessons; as he couldn't stay at home either, he went wandering round some of the roads (near where St. Andrew's church is now). During the afternoon, he saw a little girl (this

ing (as opposed to building) to which Daphne is referring.

sounds Dickensian!) pulling along a handcart with coal in it – selling it or taking it home? Having nothing to do, he picked up a pebble and tossed it towards her. Unfortunately, it hit her and she ran. A neighbour saw him from a window and told his parents and he was duly punished and cured of 'playing hooky'.

I will put together more about his family in another section – given time – but a lot can be dredged from his (and his siblings') letters from when they were young. His mother kept all their letters and they are fascinating.[8]

Back to 1924…My father had transferred to the Royal Army Pay Corps after he lost his leg, and, after their very brief honeymoon, they went to live in a rented house (upstairs flat I think) at 21B Bulstrode Road, Hounslow, London, to be near the London docks where the troopships came in, as the soldiers were paid as they disembarked. His brother, Arthur Hamilton Kelly, twelve years younger, used to visit them and we have old photos of them playing a game with tiddlywinks. (See Figure 58.) I think it was homemade and looks like a cross between Snakes and Ladders and Shove-Ha'penny. On the wall behind them are the three watercolour paintings that are now on our sitting room wall. They had bought them from a sergeant in the Pay Office (Robert Kennett? – the signature is hard to read), who wanted to be a professional painter when he retired.

Then, he was posted to Southampton to be paymaster to the returning troops there. They found a house at 85 Fairfield Road, Winchester. (See Figure 61.) No baby was started and eventually their doctor advised, 'forget about babies for a little, go for a holiday and enjoy yourselves,' so they went to Folkestone. Thereafter, they joked that it was 'all the whiting they ate on holiday that did it!', for a baby was soon on the way; on 4th May 1927 – my sister, Sheila, was born at home after a very long labour. The nurse, for a long time, just told my mother she wasn't trying hard enough and put a plank across the iron bed railing for her to brace her feet against. Eventually, she did send for the doctor who diagnosed a breech birth and turned Sheila round (leaving a red mark on one of her fingers); she was born about a month early, 3 lb. 14 oz. All the baby clothes were much too large for her, so the nurse sewed her into a cotton wool jacket. Grannie Kelly came for a visit to see her new grandchild, looked into the cot and endeared herself to no one by saying, 'She is much too small - she won't live long'.

Our mother spent almost every hour of the day and night feeding, rubbing in oil, massaging and exercising and loving, and my sister survived and flourished. She was christened Sheila Kathleen, the first because my mother had always thought she would like a daughter called Sheila and the second for our father's sister.

Almost before they had time to think about it, there was another baby on the way and our father's family all looked forward to a son, 'for the Regiment'. So, they decided on the names – Thomas Edward Conyngham, all good Kelly names – and they chose the godparents – my father's Uncle Allan (a contemporary of my grandfather); Colonel Bowen, and a godmother, Mrs. Fleming, the wife of a long retired colonel.[9] So, on 22nd

---

8   All extant letters to Daphne are in the possession of Lt. Col. CMF Randall at Westbury, Wiltshire.

9   For details of Mrs. Fleming see Chapter 8.

Figure 58. Arthur H. Kelly, Edward Kelly and Muriel playing tiddlywinks!

Figure 59. Grannie Kelly (c.1900) with Conyngham (left) and Edward (right)

Figure 60.
Father holding Sheila, late 1927/early 1928

May 1928, I was born and a second godmother was chosen, a Mrs. De'ath, also the wife of a retired colonel.

I think I was eventually taken around for inspection by godparents and Mrs. De'ath endeared herself to my mother by saying her name was pronounced 'Death' and she didn't see the point of changing spelling or pronunciation; she had married a Death and she was happy with that. I think Uncle Allan was in South Africa when I was born (see his diaries, photocopies and other notes and photos).[10] Mrs. Fleming lived at 'Raycroft,' at Lacock, near Chippenham, in Wiltshire, the first address I can remember learning to write, as she always sent me a very expensive looking Easter egg which, of course, I shared with the others at home. She preferred to remember her godchildren at Easter because it is such an important Christian festival – a view which I hope is regaining importance now.

My mother again had a difficult labour, but this time the doctor was sent for sooner and I was turned round with forceps – like Sheila, but no red marks on fingers for me; instead, there are white marks on the calf of my left leg, still just visible! I was over 7 lb. and didn't need 24-hour-a-day attention, which

---

10 As with the letters to Daphne (mentioned above), these are in the possession of Lt. Col. CMF Randall at Westbury, Wiltshire.

Figure 61. 85 Fairfield Road, Winchester The house where Shelia and Daphne Kelly were born

was fortunate as Sheila still needed a lot of attention.

It was about this time that Shelia started wearing spectacles, as she had one very 'lazy' eye which turned right inwards towards her nose. The eye specialist said she would lose the sight in it if it wasn't made to work, so she had glasses tied on with ribbon while she was a toddler, and a black patch that clipped on – one day over the good eye to make the bad one work and changed over the next day to give the good one a chance. My mother said she prayed every day for those eyes, and when Sheila was 16 the specialist said, 'You can throw away the glasses now'.

As we grew to be toddlers and during most of our childhood, Shelia was the plump, healthy looking one, and I was the thin one. Shelving the name 'Thomas', etc., they chose Daphne because they liked it and Muriel for my mother. Our Grandmother Kelly paid another state visit and this time announced, 'Well, at least she is healthy, but it is a pity it is not a boy; poor Edward is so disappointed'. 'Poor Edward,' who was in the next room and heard, spoke the only sharp words our mother ever heard him say to his mother – 'I am not disappointed and I wouldn't change my two girls for all the boys in the world'.

Figure 62. Mother holding Daphne in 1929

Chapter Six

1928-1931: China

Two and a half months (August 1928) after I was born, our father left for a year's unaccompanied posting to China.[1]

When Sheila was born, the young daughter of a friend had stayed with them for several months to help in the house, while our mother devoted herself to looking after Sheila. Now they felt they wanted some more permanent help, someone with whom they had enough in common to take to China with them, when my mother went out a year later; someone who would not be treated as a servant, but more as a friend. They had visualised someone quite young, but none of the girls they interviewed seemed suitable. Consequently, they invited one more to come for an interview. As soon as she and our mother talked, they were both convinced they need look no further. So, Miss Wood came into our lives and was immediately referred to as 'Woodie' – a cross between the formality of Miss Wood and the unheard of chance (in those days) that we might even hear her Christian name, let alone use it! I can't even remember what her Christian name was for, after coming to us, everyone called her Woodie.[2] (See Figure 64.)

She came to live in the Winchester house on her 30th birthday (19 June 1928) and was with us for getting on seven years. She was as tall and stately as my mother was small, and she

---

1 Edward's brother suggests that he departed in October 1928. (See Appendix II.) No emigration record of Edward Kelly's departure for China has been located.

2 'Woodie' was Joan Henrietta Ethel Wood (1898-1995). She was born on 19 June 1898 and died in September 1995 at Horsham, Sussex. When Muriel Kelly died in October 1957, she left her entire estate of £764 0s. 10d. to Woodie, perhaps out of gratitude and friendship, or perhaps because Woodie had few resources of her own. See *National Probate Calendar, Index of Wills and Administrations*, 1957, 32.

Figure 63. Edward Kelly by Soochow Creek, Shanghai, c.1930 (The Old German Consulate is in the background)

Figure 64. Woodie visiting Bedford in 1946

Figure 65. The Doll Painting

Figure 66. H.M.T. City of Marseilles

Figure 67. Victoria Park, Tiensin, China, 1909

Figure 68. Victorian Road, British Section, Tiensin, China, c.1930s

Figure 69. Pei-Tai-Ho, c.1903

covered considerable shyness with a manner that some people found quite intimidating. She had a sophisticated dress sense while our mother tended to the more homely. In those days, when all women wore corsets, Woodie's were incredibly boned, and being cuddled by her could be quite painful! What one suffers for fashion! Woodie had been a dutiful daughter to her parents in Sussex for many years, but was glad of the chance to travel, as well as live in a loving home. (Aunt Elsie Birkett, longing for a career, had done much the same years before and gone to Burma as a nanny;[3] after a tour there, she went to India with another family, returning to England during World War I.)

The day my father went to China, he went into the bedroom to say goodbye to me in my cot and came out and said to my mother, 'She really smiled at me – I know she will remember me'. Our father sent photos of China and of himself, and he painted watercolour pictures of places which he sent back, too. He also sent Sheila a little doll from China and painted a watercolour picture of it (See Figure 65.) and himself and a dragon to represent China, and how the doll was coming over the sea to her. (It is now in the green folder I made while

---

3 Which perhaps explains why Harold Birkett went out to the Far East (i.e., Borneo) to farm after completing his course at Wye College.

Chapter Six ~ 1928-1931: China

Figure 70. The Beach at Pei-Tai-Ho, c.1919

at college, along with other watercolours by various family members more talented than me.)[4]

At the end of a year, my mother and Woodie packed up their personal belongings, left the furnished house in Winchester and sailed for China on the troopship, *H.M.T. City of Marseilles*.[5] (See Figure 66.) What Woodie had not told my parents, however, was that she was a very poor sailor; even to look at the sea could make her feel bad. She tried hard to overcome her affliction, but was not much help during the voyage as my mother toiled about with the two of us. Sheila could toddle on land, but gave up when the ship was at sea.

The voyage took seven weeks and was the first troopship to go to the Far East through the Panama Canal. The ship was mainly full of the Argyll and Sutherlands. It stopped at various places to refill with coal (coolies

---

4 Typical self-deprecation by DMR. (CMFR).
5 The *H.M.T. City of Marseilles* had a long and colorful history. It was a ship of 8,250 gross tons, length 469' x beam 57', one funnel, two masts, twin screws and a speed of 13 knots. It had accommodation for 141 first and 46 second-class passengers. It was built by Palmers Shipbuilding Company of Newcastle, and launched in October 1912. Her maiden voyage began on January 26, 1913 when she left Liverpool for New York, Port Said and Bombay; she subsequently ran on the Liverpool - Bombay service. On November 23, 1915 she was attacked by a German submarine, but returned fire and drove it off. In November 1916 she picked up 95 survivors from the P&O Line ship Arabia, which had been torpedoed near Cape Matapan (or Cape Tainaron, off southern Greece). In 1921 she was used on the American & Indian Line's service between New York, Port Said and Bombay, and later via Marseilles and Naples. In 1923, she was employed for regular seasonal trooping work to India. On 6 January 1940 she was damaged by a mine off the River Tay and, on 22 January 1943, ran aground at Ceylon, but was refloated. She was finally scrapped in 1947.

running up planks with baskets on their heads!) and passengers went ashore to escape the dust and, as in Woodie's case, to recover from seasickness. One of the few times she felt able to come up on deck, she sank into a deck chair which promptly collapsed on her thumb. Another time, she got a cinder in her eye and, by the end of the voyage, she was quite well known to the doctor! Even their free day in Bermuda was full of excitement as Sheila walked off the edge of the swimming pool into the water and disappeared except for her topee. My mother jumped in and saved her. Both had been fully dressed. We were often told about the alligators on the other side of the net which fenced the pool from the sea, the monkeys in the trees and the vultures flying overhead! And those topees! Never was the sun allowed to touch our heads and there we are in the old photos like two little mushrooms![6] Years later, I made little cotton sunhats for our children in Malaya, though most people didn't use any covering on their children at all.

After seven weeks of looking after two children and Woodie, our mother was thankful when we reached Shanghai. Then, there was just an overnight train journey to Tientsin, trying to sleep on the shiny leather-padded seats and slipping off occasionally. Our father met the train and later he said he had never before seen four such worn out, dirty females get off a train. But no matter, they were reunited at last.

Figure 71. Muriel in a Rickshaw in Tientsin, c.1931

I can remember a little of those next two years – the No. 1 houseboy and the cook who used to pass us peanuts through the serving hatch till my mother found out and told us not to accept them as they might not be clean. I wonder what happened to No. 1 houseboy. I hope he didn't suffer under the communists because he had worked for the 'capitalists'. I remember him when we left, running down the station platform, waving to us after his last pleas to come with us and look after us for always![7] I can remember the sitting room, the part that had the sofa anyway. My mother and Woodie had gone out together (they rarely did) to a ladies' party of some sort,[8] and our father played 'growly bears' round the sofa and chairs. What a surprise when he moved the sofa to make more room

---

6   Sadly, no such photos have been found. (CMFR)

7   We had the same sad farewell when we left Malaya in 1962. My faithful Indian boot boy insisted he would look after us and would sleep on a mat outside the front door in England! (CMFR)

8   Curiously, the Scottish missionary and 1924 Olympic Gold Medalist Eric Liddell (of Chariots of Fire fame) was also in Tientsin during much of the same time as the Kellys. Liddell taught at the Anglo-Chinese College and was superintendent of the Sunday School at the Union Church, where his father officiated. He lived on Cambridge Road. One cannot help but wonder if their paths crossed in the small, tight-knit British community at Tientsin.

Figure 72. H.M.T. Neuralia

Figure 73. HMT Neuralia on the Whangpoo River off Shanghai, 8 November 1929

for himself behind it! I had, till then, thought that all furniture was immovable!

In the summer times, we went further north to Pei-Tai-Ho which was then a collection of little holiday homes for ex-pats.[9] (See Figures 69 and 70.) (In the modern spelling, the region is called Beidaihe, east of Beijing. In the dreadful communist years, Mao had himself a vast holiday home built there, and other communist chiefs had lesser homes built around.) I can remember being carried through the scratchy bushes from the bungalow (See Figure 74.) down to the beach, and being told at some stage that I was big enough to walk through the bushes by myself and carry at least one of my beach toys. Usually, by the time we reached the beach, it had been cleared of the line of dead jellyfish that the tide seemed to strand every night. Occasionally, the beach clearer was late and our mother and Woodie, with sticks, pushed the horrible jellyfish aside so we could get to the sea to paddle. By the time we left China, I could almost swim, but only backwards for some reason! Our father stayed in Tientsin and came to Pei-Tai-Ho for weekends during the holiday. We must have gone sightseeing together, but just once we were left with Woodie for several days while our parents went to Peking. Some part of the journey was done on donkeys and we were considered too small for such an expedition. (Did my father really ride a donkey with one false leg?)

The two years in China were not easy for our parents. Sheila had caught scarlet fever while we were out there and, for a while, they thought she would not survive. She was isolated so that they were allowed only to wave to her through a window. Her temperature went so high that one of her eardrums burst and the doctor punctured the other to save it from bursting. After one of their visits to the hospital, they came home to find Woodie encouraging me to eat a little of my supper (of scrambled egg, I think), but I couldn't swallow. My tonsils had caught my share of the scarlet fever and I was rushed off to hospital, where they were taken out. I don't remember the hospital, but I can still see the expression on Woodie's face as she turned to my parents as they came through the door and she said, 'She really is trying!', and the appalled look on my parents' faces.

The Chinese servants were convinced that a devil had got into the house because our parents had not allowed them to put a mirror over the front door, which would have frightened any devil so much that he would have fled. When Sheila was brought home and carried into the house, the servants all came out to welcome her, probably hoping that she was not bringing any little devils back with her. Do I remember it or is it just imagining

---

9 English railway engineers were the first Europeans to 'discover' the fishing village of Pei-Tai-Ho during the 1890s. The families of foreign missionaries serving in inland China made good use of the area beginning around 1900, as did many wealthy Chinese and foreign diplomats from Peking and Tianjin. The village was severely damaged by Hurricane Barbour in 1934.

Figure 74. The Bungalow in Pei-Tai-Ho by Edward Kelly, 1929

their smiling faces and little clapping hands?

The other incident I can partly remember is when Sheila, being dried after her bath, dropped a doll's china teacup into the bath in which I was still standing, watching the water go down the plughole. The cup shattered and a splinter went into the front of my ankle which bled dramatically. Wrapping my foot in one towel and the rest of me in another, my mother carried me out of the house to our friendly rickshaw man, who squatted in the gutter just up the road with his friends while waiting for business; he helped us into his rickshaw and did his best-ever time to the hospital, where I was told to bite my thumb while iodine was poured into the cut. After bandaging my foot, they had to anoint the thumb as well!

Speaking of rickshaw men, my father had his special one who took him to the office every day. One day, he went out and saw the rickshaw men squatting in their little circle as usual, but all roaring with laughter. On going closer, my father saw 'his' man dripping blood from a gash on his head. The man was ready to pull my father as usual, but my father insisted he went to the nearest hospital and was attended to. We were told of this incident as an illustration of the different ways that other cultures show their sympathy. I remember their dusty, ragged clothes and their lined, apparently aged, faces, but they were probably quite young. Most rickshaw men were said to die young through straining their hearts, and some customers only chose men who pulled faster than others. I know we always left plenty of time for our journeys, as we didn't like to hear the poor men panting and labouring. I wish I could remember more, but when we went to Malaya, about 30 years later, the first time I went into a town and smelled the Chinese food stalls, I remembered the smells as though it had been the day before (and there were no Chinese 'take-aways' in England then that could have reminded me). I suppose that is kinetic memory, but baby Wendy on my arm felt for an instant all wrong – it should have been me on the adult's arm. I do think it is good to live in another culture when one is little; it gives one an empathy for ways and thoughts not naturally one's own, and you realize that the world is made up of more than your own street and town.

Somewhere, I have a postcard picture of the *City of Marseilles* and of the *Neuralia*[10] on which we came home. (See Figures 66, 72 and 73.) There is also a watercolour by my father of the bungalow in Pei-Tai-Ho. (See Figure 74.)

This painting doesn't show the part of the garden where I can remember my sister and me playing. It was one of the few places where we were allowed to walk by ourselves, theoretically in sight of our mother or Woodie sitting on the veranda, but 'out of sight' depended on the height of the flowers. They were not at all pleased with me when, presumably not long out of nappies and desperate to get back to the house, I hid behind a small bush while Sheila kept lookout, frantically telling me the gardener was looking our way! The silhouette of that bush and the gardener far away up the path, hoeing, is one of my memory pictures!

It seems strange to me that I can't remember anything about the voyage home on the Neuralia, except that at least some of the voyage was rough and it was difficult to stay upright when trying to play on the deck. Though we had gone out through the Panama Canal, we came home through the Suez. Once, the ship lurched very suddenly and I rolled into the scuppers and was soaked. As I rolled, I saw my father's feet come off the deck and then come down again over me. He had been leaning on the rail, looking out to sea and came dangerously near going right over the rail. My mother threw herself out of her deck chair and grabbed me with one hand and my father's ankle with the other. She remarked afterwards, 'I thought, at least we'll go together'.

---

10 The *Neuralia* was the sister ship of the *HMT Nevasa*. It had been built in 1912 in Glasgow as a passenger liner for the British India Line. At the outbreak of World War I, however, she was quickly converted for service as a troopship, as the prefix H.M.T. suggests. She undertook passenger duties and educational cruises between the wars, but returned to troopship duties in World War II. She survived several U-boat attacks, but was finally sunk in the Gulf of Taranto by an Italian mine on May 1st, 1945, with the loss of 4 lives.

Chapter Seven

1931-1934:
Leamington Spa

No more inner pictures or kinetic memories for a while! When we reached England, I suppose we went by train to Bedford for disembarkation leave. My father's father had died while we were in China,[1] but his mother still lived in Bedford. She must still have been at 29, Kimbolton Road (See Figure 76.) because I do remember the rather overgrown, shrubby front garden and the gate on the corner with Kimbolton Avenue. There may have been another gate straight onto Kimbolton Road so carriages could go in one and out the other. There are two photocopied pictures of the house in the collection Apphia sent to me a while ago.

There were some lovely old toys there, including a model shop with little plaster hams and joints of meat to hang from hooks on the ceiling and plaster groceries to arrange on the counter. To reach this comfortably, I was allowed to sit on a high kitchen stool at the old dresser in the kitchen where it was warm. In retrospect, was this really concern for my well-being, or were we kept out of sight and sound part of the day in order 'not to tire Granny'? Granny Kelly (born 1858) must have been about 62 then,[2] but seemed

---

[1] Thomas James Pearce Kelly (1853-1930), Daphne's paternal grandfather, died on 23 July 1930 at 29 Kimbolton Road, Bedford. He served in the 44th Regiment of Foot (mostly in India and Burma), and retired as a Lieutenant-Colonel on 3 December 1890. From May 1915 until July 1917, he returned to the Army to serve on the Recruiting Staff at Braintree, Essex. At the time of his death, his estate was valued at probate at over £8,800.

[2] In fact she would have been 73 in 1931! (CMFR) According to extant records in Canada and England, Fanny Kelly (née Loosemore), Daphne's paternal grandmother, was born on 12 September 1859 in Prince William, New Brunswick, Canada, the daughter of the Revd Philip Wood Loosemore, the Rector of Prince William, and his wife Elizabeth Isabella Loosemore. In the 1871 Census, the family was living in Aldborough, Yorkshire, where Mr. Loosemore was Vicar of the parish church.

incredibly old and always dressed in black.

I can remember being told that Sheila, Woodie and I were left in Bedford for a few days while our parents went to Leamington to find a house for us to live in for the three-year posting to the Pay Office in Warwick. In those days, army families rented their own accommodation, and I don't remember any mention of army quarters till the later 1930s when Leslie Hore-Belisha (Liberal MP and Secretary of State for War, 1937-1940) had the majority of army quarters built. 'Why did families only have a quarter of a house', I wondered when I was older? My parents had had crates of furniture shipped back from China; we still have some here and there and Sheila has some small pieces. The carved camphor wood chest has gone to Muriel and Cameron; the plain chest with divisions and green baize lining was specially built to bring back the silver and small ivory pieces. My parents believed in few, but good (rather than heaps of 'tourist quality') ornaments. (See Figure 77.)

They had made (to the design of my father) a large blue carpet with dragons in each corner and two matching rugs to save wear and tear in front of an open fireplace, or another much trodden area. For a dining room, they had bought a readymade beige carpet with the Chinese 'good luck' symbol round the edges. One large and two small occasional tables had folding ebony legs, round brass tops and a lower tray. As packing round the carpets, there were several rush (or bamboo) mats, and until we could afford carpets in the bedrooms, we used these instead. They were cold on my father's foot while he struggled into his false leg every morning, so they bought a tiny blue and grey foot mat to go beside his bed. (Wendy has it now.)

My parents rented 47a, Kenilworth Road in Leamington and, from various shops I suppose, they ordered other essential furniture and items, such as the two saucepans which I still have (much to the amusement of David and Jess!). It turned into a bit of a joke that my mother would say how she would buy some thicker, better quality saucepans when they could afford them; we never did, though many years later a few were inherited from someone. I suppose they also bought the little car we had in Leamington, but it must have taken a while to have the clutch and brake put onto one pedal so my father could work that and the accelerator with his one foot.

While they were moving everything in, a lot of the local tradesmen called hoping for regular orders. A lot of shops then delivered to the home – milk, fish, meat, groceries. On their delivery rounds, they watched to see signs of 'moving in' and then called at the door. 47a was the back (i.e., servants') part of a large house that fronted onto a road just round the corner. There is a photo of it taken years later when we were driving through Leamington on a holiday, the year Charles came with us and we went to York as well. (See Figure 79.)

Figure 75. Daphne in 1931

Figure 76. 'Mount Vernon', 29 Kimbolton Road, Bedford, c.1922 in summer and winter

I have in my mind an image of Sheila, Woodie and me in the front garden looking back at the house. But what I was really wondering at was the flat paving stones, so regular, so clean, so bare compared to Chinese road-gutters, and solid roads right across to the other pavement! There was a space between the double hedge along the front of the property that small people could creep along. For a while, we could only play in the front garden with the big gate firmly shut. This was because there was an ancient elm tree in the back garden which was pronounced unsafe, and soon after we moved in a man came and felled it. We were allowed to scramble among the fallen branches and enjoyed playing shipwrecks till it was all cleared away.

Then my father started gardening in earnest and we had to mind the flowerbeds! The front garden sloped down from the road to the garage, which was under the large bedroom that for a while we shared with Woodie. The front door was in the centre and the dining room window to its left. There was a flowerbed contained by a low wall outside the dining room, and the slope of the ground meant that the bed was on ground level on its other side where it met the gravel of the turning space. Several little brick steps were at the end of the wall and, if one went up them, we could see into the next garden – not encouraged, as it was rude to peep. We used to have a picture

Figure 77. Two of the carved ivory pieces, which we still have. The 'lady' is 21cm tall and the 'puzzle' is 5.5cm square

of the front of 47a, all decorated with paper pompoms and flags, either for the jubilee of George V or the accession of Edward VIII, the first I think.

Inside the front door was black and white lino down the long narrow passage – how different to current times when wall-to-wall carpeting is usual and so many things that people consider essential now were then luxuries, if they were even thought of at all! This front door may have been an addition when the house was divided because it opened into a very long passage, the whole depth of the house, ending at what must have been the original back door, with the stairs on the left and beside them the door to the cellars.

Those cellar rooms could have been graded in standards of bravery! Down the brick steps and turn right and one was in the larder (no 'fridges' in those days). There was a raised brick 'bench' all round and perhaps a yard deep. Obviously intended for use by a large household, our dairy produce sat in one section and, sometimes, one or both of us would be asked to go down and bring up some easy-to-carry object, like a packet of butter. Down the steps and turn left and one had to get a good grip of one's imagination to go right into the room, very faintly lit by a small dirty window high up on the front wall. Here our mother kept bowls of bulbs until their shoots were advanced enough for them to come up

Figure 78. It is not mentioned in the narrative, but these newspaper cuttings show the Birketts in 1931 on their Golden Wedding anniversary. Auntie Mary is in the centre and Aunt Elsie is on the right. I assume the others are Norman (who lost a leg in the war) and his family.

to the warmth and light. The final test of one's bravery was to walk through the bulb room and into the entrance of the completely dark room off it. This was where the coal was kept, arriving at interesting intervals on a cart pulled by a horse and being humped on dirty shoulders across the drive and shot down a hatch. When playing in the front garden, it was almost unbelievable to look at the outside of the hatch and the window, standing in the sun and wondering why one had to be so brave when inches away on the other side in the dark!

In the entrance passage, opposite the cellar door and stairs, was a coat rack or pegs (or both), and on one of these our father hung his greatcoat. It seemed so heavy and stiff to us that we used to hold it round the middle and try to heave it up to catch on its peg – without it touching the floor of course. It seemed ages before I could do that.

Up a half flight of stairs and the kitchen was on the right – more black and white lino! No fitted units in those days. A wooden table stood opposite the door and the kitchen window looked out over the little yard and down the garden. There was also a wooden draining board and a sink. In the corner to the right of the door there was a small fuelled stove with a slow cooker, where my father's staple rice pudding was almost always cooking. The stove also heated the bathwater and there was a

Figure 79. 47a Kenilworth Road, Leamington Spa in March 1990

gas cooker somewhere. There was a cupboard on the landing outside the kitchen door, and on top of this our father hung a gong made from a WWI shell case. This was sounded to tell everyone upstairs that it was time to wash their hands and come down for meals. If we were good and quick we might be lifted up to sound it again.

The gong was next to the dining room door and, once opened, it required two steps down – something that visitors were always warned about! The dining room window looked onto the little raised flowerbed with its little brick edge, so tempting for anyone who had an irresistible urge to climb on anything remotely climbable – though not Auntie Sheila. I don't remember ever falling off or out of anything, so why did everyone fuss so much? On one occasion, Sheila fell out of a Syringa tree at the back of the house and cut her leg a bit on the way down. I was twice as high but came down alright (as always) but, after that, there was no more climbing in that tree. When I was a bit older, I could climb over the wall at the bottom of the back garden (easy if you stand on the rubbish heap), and stand in the little dusty lane, which occasionally a farmer used to get into a field on the far side of the lane. I took care not to tell any adults about my climbing over. It was more difficult to get back without skinning your knees or dirtying your clothes. Eventually, I grew and it was so easy to do that I didn't bother with it anymore.

The sitting room, or our father's 'den', contained the little yacht piano, (See Figure 80.) a table for his painting, a chair and bookcase, and the truly vast 'cloakroom' with the only loo in the house, which was up the lino-covered stairs.

Our father used the hand basin in the cloakroom to shave in the mornings, leaving the bathroom up on the next floor for the womenfolk. His leather strop hung by the basin and his razor was on the shelf, as we were thought to be old enough to be trusted never to touch it and we didn't. If we dressed and got ready for going down to breakfast quickly, we could sit on the stairs and listen for the sound of the razor being sharpened on the strop and know that he would come out right after.

This cloakroom had a very big built-in airing-cupboard and another un-warmed cupboard and a stack of packing boxes. Now the army provides the boxes for packing, but back then we had to have our own and, being specially made, they were always kept somewhere ready for the next move.[3] After a while, I was allowed to have a table in there for putting out my farm toys and soldiers, and sometimes, as a special treat, my father's soldiers. (See Figure 81.)

Up another half flight of stairs was the bathroom, another apparently huge room. Turn left and up the second half of those stairs and onto a landing were the three bedrooms, the first one on the right was our parents' bedroom, the next one on the right was our bedroom, and, straight ahead, was the spare room. The landing was big enough for us to have one of the large packing cases – shelves made by our father and a curtain across the front – for a toy cupboard.

Next to that and under the window which looked onto the back garden, was a seat made from an outgrown cot. Our mother made cushions for it and we used to sit there and read our books. Once, I made Sheila crouch down against the wall, covered her with some dressing-up clothes, and told

Figure 80. The yacht piano at The Cedars, Westbury, Wiltshire, in 2010.

The lower panel hinges down to reveal the five-octave keyboard. The portrait above is of Daphne's Great Grandfather, General Thomas Conyngham Kelly CB, 1808-1887. On the piano is a picture of Daphne winning the shooting competition at my unit's annual 'family day'! (CMFR)

---

3 We still had to have our own for most of our many moves from the 1950s to the 1970s, and some of the boxes were the same solid, well-made Kelly ones. A couple of these boxes are still in use as cupboards in the garage. (CMFR)

Chapter Seven ~ 1931-1934: Leamington Spa

Figure 81. A few of the large collection of lead figures, much treasured, dating from about 1900 to about 1940. Happily, they are still in the family

her it would make our mother laugh if I said I couldn't find Sheila. I sat on her to make it even more convincing. My little joke didn't work out as planned, however; maybe coming up all those stairs didn't help her sense of humour because all she said was, 'Why are you sitting on Sheila? How many times have I told you to be careful of her glasses!' I wasn't sitting on her head, but – you've guessed – I had bent them.

In our bedroom, we had two 'camp' beds, each with solid wooden frame, wire base and a folding head end. When we were tucked up for the night, one of our amusements was to squeeze ourselves under these bars. Of course, as we grew it became a tighter squeeze, and eventually one of us thought we were stuck forever and the other had to call downstairs for help. That was not popular, and it signalled the end of that pastime!

A safer game was me telling Sheila stories, using my fingers as little people. Each finger had a different name. I remember 'Narnkypoo' and 'Pop'. They can't have been very exciting stories because sometimes she used to go to sleep in the middle of them. In winters, the landing grew too cold for playing and we had a table in a corner of the dining room where we could write and play 'offices'. The many Vernons and Littlewoods pools forms that came through the door gave us hours of occupation, convinced that we were doing office work with sums like our father, by filling those tiny squares with ticks and numbers.

At some stage, we had been allowed to see our father's office in the Warwick R.A.P.C. building, which had once been a country house and was surrounded by a very large garden where there was an annual families' garden party. (See Figure 82.)

His room was the one with the 'joke' bookcase on the back of the door,[4] and not much else in it except his desk and chair. If there were filing cabinets or cupboards, I don't remember them. It was a hard wooden chair and my mother made a cushion for the seat and a little one that tied to the back of the chair with tapes. His false leg was heavy metal and, I think, was kept in place with a belt and strap over his shoulder, and the cushions eased the discomfort and backache. He never complained about it, as far as I remember. There was also a tiny mat to keep the drafts off the good leg.

The office must have been as cold in winter as our house, for there was no double-glazing in those days, or central heating. There was no heating in the bedrooms either, except during the worst winter days when our mother would light a very small oil stove a few minutes before we had to get up and dress. I suppose Woodie lit the one in our bedroom (which she shared) until she left. Under the Chinese rush/bamboo mats there were just stained floorboards. Our parents' room was the same except for the tiny blue and grey mat. Our father wore 'stump socks', which our mother knitted in white wool. If he lost weight, he wore two to stop the false leg rubbing. (In 1947, he wrote to us from Jerusalem that he had got so thin that he was wearing four layers of socks and was thinking he might have to send one of his two false legs back to London to be altered. I don't think he ever did.)

Children accept their parents as the norm and I thought all fathers, the really special, good ones, had only one leg! (Our Uncle Norman Birkett had one leg; after about 20 operations that he underwent as the result of a wound he received at the end of WWI, his leg had to be amputated.) When our father watered the garden, he took a manhole cover off an old well in the little courtyard and let the watering can down on a rope. He held onto the side fence while he did this, and often our mother would be looking anxiously out of the kitchen window, fearful that he might topple into the well. I must say, his false leg did look unreliable as he put it out sideways and straight. He liked a walk round the garden when he came back from the office and, if he was really tired, he would go upstairs first and 'take his leg off'. Then he would go round the garden using his crutches; his flapping trouser leg safely pinned up. He still managed to look well dressed.

There was a large brick potting shed in the garden, quite near the house, on the edge

---

[4] The office is now part of the Royal Warwickshire Fusiliers Museum building, which we visited a few years ago and the 'book-case door' is still there. (CMFR)

Chapter Seven ~ 1931-1934: Leamington Spa

Figure 82. Garden Party, 1935. Parents are far right (1&2) Daphne and Sheila are on the far table, right, backs to the camera either side of large hat!

of the little courtyard near the garage. On the garden side of the shed there was a privet hedge, presumably planted when the garden was its original size. To 'help' our father with the gardening, my older sister was eventually trusted to use the shears on this hedge. I was upset that I was not allowed to use the shears, not even 'in turns', so I fetched my little blunt-ended paper scissors and just about kept pace with her. The effort raised a strange lump on one finger between the first two joints and, to this day, if I use stiff scissors for long, the swelling reappears.

In China, I suppose we had become used to a certain amount of begging, but I can remember being surprised when a tramp first came to our door in England. What mark they put outside we never discovered, but word seemed to get round that father was a soft touch for a (money) handout, or mother for a little food to help them on their way. If our father thought anyone was particularly deserving, he would do more, believing their sorrowful tales of joblessness, and he would try to get them little odd jobbing or gardening work with his friends. They had a tendency to disappear, however, only to reappear when the money was spent.

One in particular, whose name was Walton, reappeared with monotonous regularity. He usually smelt, but my mother would give him a cup of tea, and once we were told to take the cup and saucer to the potting shed where he sat on a chair and rested till our father came home. He thanked us and then launched into a long sentence of which neither of us could understand a word. At the end, we smiled and nodded and said 'Yes', so that we were not impolite, and he looked surprised and poured some of the tea into the saucer and offered it to us, whereupon our efforts at politeness ended and we bolted to the house. Walton was eventually found lodgings in the town, given one of our father's suits, and found a job as a messenger/odd job man at the Warwick office. After a short time, he disappeared and came back after a while when he had used his pay and sold the suit! When we moved to York, he promised to visit us, but it was a long walk, and when we moved to Bedford three months later, he must have lost track of us, mercifully.

There were, even then, many out-of-work servicemen; some would get together in a little group, and if they could in any degree play a musical instrument, they would stand around in towns playing with varying degrees of skill. Begging was against the law, but apparently there was no law against just standing and playing musical instruments. Once, we passed a group too far away to give them money, but seeing our father's walking stick and straight leg, and presuming it had been a war wound (he _was_ wounded, twice, but the leg was 1922), they quickly switched to playing 'Old Soldiers Never Die' and I was sent back with a handful of change.

Chapter Eight

1934-1937:
Extended time in Leamington, and School

Our father's posting to the Warwick office was to last three years. As time was running short, but with no news of his next posting, Woodie and my mother began sorting and thinning the accumulation of the past three years. In the end, the powers-that-be decided he should have another three years at Warwick, so the boxes were unpacked and we settled down again.

Originally, we had tiny Mickey Mouse tricycles and were happy taking our feet off the pedals and careening down the front drive. Sometimes, our mother would open the garage door before our father came home and we would have competitions to see which of us could roll down the slope into the garage, keeping to one side, and see who could get round the furthest. When we were settled back into Leamington for the second three years, we were given larger three-wheelers and were able to careen down the front slope even faster, occasionally turning too close to the (shut) garage door, which left marks on both the door and me!

On rainy days, we might be allowed to play shipwrecks in the garage or under the covered pathway to the back garden (low and cobwebby). A few years ago, Sheila reminded me of the game 'shipwrecks', and said how surprised she was that we were allowed to climb up and all over probably wobbly constructions in a garage that had a concrete floor. Probably she didn't scramble about as much as I did or she might well have fallen off.

While Woodie was with us, she and our mother took turns to take us for an afternoon walk. Sometimes, when we were bigger, we would almost reach the outskirts of Warwick. Walks with Woodie tended to be slightly longer, but not nearly as interesting as with our mother who would chat about trees and plants and all sorts of things and, when the pavements and paths were covered with fallen leaves, she would let us scuff along kicking our 'rainfalls' of leaves, even if it did spoil the toes of our shoes!

Figure 83. Daphne's father by the garage door in Leamington in 1937, so it must be the larger version of the tricycle that is visible!

Originally, Woodie was going to be with us only while we were in China, but she became so much a part of the family that she stayed on for some time while we lived in Leamington. Before she came to us, she had had no specific training and looked after her mother who lived in Sussex. After her time with us, she worked as a nanny or looked after old ladies for the rest of her working life. I remember her coming to Bedford to visit; one of her visits there occurred after I had bought a car, and she and our mother were delighted to be taken for a drive. She called our parents (as a lot of people did) Bruv and Moosie. (Bruv was the nearest to Edward that his brother Arthur, James and Apphia's father, could get when Arthur was learning to talk – he was 12 years our father's junior.) Woodie was one of those people who are almost incapable of writing a letter: eventually, we had to assume she had died.

Sheila had several operations on her ear/ears while we were in Leamington, possibly to close the holes in her eardrums. We were told she would be deaf in both ears without the ops., and she was afterwards in a nursing home, which was quite a walk from Warwick New Road, because I remember walking to see her; I also recall the peonies our father picked from the garden to take to her, as Sheila said then they were her favourite flowers. They grew at the bottom of the garden near the rubbish pile where I used to climb over the end wall, and so did Solomon's Seal – which was always covered in 'cuckoo spit'.

Sheila also had many visits to the eye specialist, as her lenses were frequently

Chapter Eight ~ 1934-1937: Extended time in Leamington, and School

Figure 84. New College (School), Leamington in 1936. Miss Raley is in the centre, Daphne is front row, far right (properly uniformed!) and Sheila is second row, sixth from left.

changed to help her lazy eye. She wore glasses till she was 16. She looked strange without them at first, but her eyes were straight, though she says she knows she looks at things with her 'good' eye unless she consciously uses two.

Sheila started school when she was seven, which was usual then. Up the road towards Warwick a little way, turn left, and the first big old house just across that road was the school.[1] There were joint headmistresses, Miss Raley and Miss Chambers, the latter very thin with straight bobbed hair and very shy. Miss Raley had wavy hair and was plumper. They had seen us playing in the front garden and when we looked about the age to start school, Miss Raley called on our mother one afternoon and asked if, when they were considering schools for us, would they think about theirs. She said she had never 'canvassed' for pupils before, but had seen us often and felt we would all suit each other very well!

My mother was just saying that she would have to talk it all over with her husband as the fees would probably be more than we could afford, when our father came back from the office and he and Miss Raley immediately recognised each other. She and her sister, from their youth in Bedford, had been friends with our Auntie Kathleen. So, it was decided that Sheila would go for full fees and when I started it would be for slightly less.

The 'Bedford' Miss Raley lived in the next road to Richmond Road, and when we moved to Bedford she became one of our mother's most valued friends. She was the head of

---

1 New College (School), 61 Kenilworth Road, Leamington Spa. In 1977 it merged with two other schools to form North Leamington School, a mixed comprehensive.

Bedford High School's junior department. For years Miss Raley looked after her increasingly bedridden mother; she brought our mother the first lilac blossoms from her garden and, in later years, gave both Sheila and myself a book every Christmas. Books were all I ever wanted for Christmas and Miss Raley's books were always wonderful, adventurous and mind-stretching. We were forbidden to tell any of our school friends that she was a friend of our mother's, but the predicament never arose, as we were older than the junior school children when we started at Bedford High School.

Back to Leamington....! As soon as Sheila started school I wanted to go as well, but ever mindful that she was that one year and three weeks older than me, they wanted her to start first. So, I expect I moaned and grizzled and moped about until they compromised and it was arranged that I could go to the twice-weekly band and music classes.

At first, my mother walked with me to the corner of the smaller road and saw me across and watched me go into the drive of the school. From then on, I was on my own. I had to go in and hang my coat on a peg, go up the back stairs and tap on the classroom door. Easy…no: I had a wild imagination and the shrubs at the side of the drive were huge and dark. Sometimes, children looked at me out of a window and later asked me why I didn't have a school hat, or why was I so late? The teacher rarely heard my terrified tap on the door and, sometimes, I would despair and slide in and stand by the wall, not infrequently so silently that the teacher didn't notice me for what seemed like years. Eventually, I would be found a place on a mat and given an instrument, usually the jingle bells, occasionally a triangle. We had to sound our instruments according to the coloured notes on the blackboard as the teacher pointed to each line. There were several lines for each instrument and I found it difficult at first and it all looked a terrifying jumble, but I learned fast to be like everyone else who seemed to know what they were doing. The final horrors came after the music lesson, when it was home time and we all went to the cloakroom and some of the children asked me why I had no uniform and was I very poor? I was glad when the term ended and I started fulltime with my uniform – which gave one a certain anonymity.

There was one other weekly torture: the dancing class in a huge hall in the town. Some of the boarders from the school went, marched down two and two by the matron, but most were taken by a parent, and they all sat round the hall watching unless they wanted to get off unencumbered and visit the shops. Sheila, said always to be the shy one, changed her shoes and skipped into the crowd of little girls – and a few unfortunate boys. I fiddled with my shoes and did everything possible to stay at my mother's feet. The dancing mistress would take my hand and insert me into a group of happy prancers, and my legs would go stiff with horror. I could dance by myself at home, or in the garden with Sheila, but not with all those strangers watching.

I didn't like parties either, except in one house where the granny knew that some people didn't like playing party games or joining in 'Sir Roger de Coverley' or anyone else's dance, but that they love a quiet play behind a large chair, setting out their hostess's small farm toys and peeping out at the prancers and dancers. I went cheerfully to that home whenever invited. That granny, whose name I have ungratefully forgotten, must have been quite a person. Her small granddaughter lived with them while her older granddaughter was with the parents and enduring operations and skin grafts while she recovered from setting fire to herself from a Christmas tree, while acting the part of Father Christmas. She was 14 and considered old enough to be careful near the lighted candles. Some part of her costume went up suddenly and her face was only saved from burns as someone grabbed a rug, threw her onto the floor, pressing the rug round and put out the flames. At various times, the grandmother disappeared to donate another piece of skin for grafting. Eventually, the girl recovered with her face and head unscarred.

We were invited to tea quite often by

Figure 85. Daphne's Godmother's house, 'Raycroft' and the stream where the boat was sailed in Lacock, Wiltshire, (approximately 13 miles north of Westbury, Wiltshire).
Photographed in 2010 by CMFR.

another little girl — an only child — whose parents must have been amongst the wealthiest in the area; her parents seemed invisible and she was cared for fulltime by a nanny. (This was not at all the same as having Woodie, who was one of the family!) We had tea alone in a huge dining room and were waited on by a uniformed maid. After tea, we returned to the playroom where every expensive toy imaginable was available, but rarely touched. Despite a life-sized washable baby doll with its own miniature cakes of soap and real baby bath, home was preferable! Just once I remember, when we were older, we went in the garden to try to ride her cycle, which seemed large. (We had been longing for two-wheelers, but the end of our second tour was approaching when, once again, things had to be thinned out, not accumulated, so we just got on with performing circus tricks on the old tricycles which didn't do them or us any good!) She was not allowed to go on the lawn, but that time, with no one apparently watching, she encouraged us to try riding on the grass as it was less painful when we fell or collapsed off. I think the nanny must have been watching from a window or the gardener saw the minor damage to the lawn because we were not invited to try cycling a second time.

One day, the headmistress asked which of us were going to the local pantomime. Only one hand failed to go up, the local curate's daughter. When we told our parents, they mentioned it to Miss Raley and were told that the child's mother was dead and the curate probably couldn't afford a ticket (the child was at the school for a very small nominal fee). Sheila and I were dispatched across the road and up towards the school to the flat where they lived. We were shown up the stairs by a daily housekeeper who had answered the door; the difference between their lino stairs and ours was that theirs had holes and, though I didn't know what poverty was, I sensed it all around. As usual, when we had to speak to anyone, Sheila pushed me in front of her. The curate and his daughter were having their tea at a table that apparently served as his desk, as well. The curate looked up and he had the most lovely smile, and somehow one was accepted as one was and it was so easy to deliver the message (maybe we had a written one as well). So one's circle outside home began to expand and life became more enjoyable.

We had been brought up from the earliest age not to make a fuss if we fell down or otherwise hurt ourselves – soldiers didn't make a fuss, so we should be like them – soldiers didn't cry (actually not true in all cases), so we shouldn't. One day, during school playtime, which took place in the big front drive if it was too wet to go on the grass at the back, a large girl ran into me and we both fell onto our knees. I got up and looked and listened in amazement as the girl lay on the ground screaming. She wouldn't get up and continued to scream, while the teacher looked at the small graze on her knee and finally helped her up and to the cloakroom, and the matron was summoned to deal with the little wound. She was still seeing to her when we were lined up at the end of break time and taken through the cloakroom. My knee, by this time, was a nasty mess of gravel well embedded and blood oozing around and starting to trickle down, despite my efforts at smearing it off. So I went to the matron and said, 'My knee is bleeding a little bit too' because, as I said to my mother

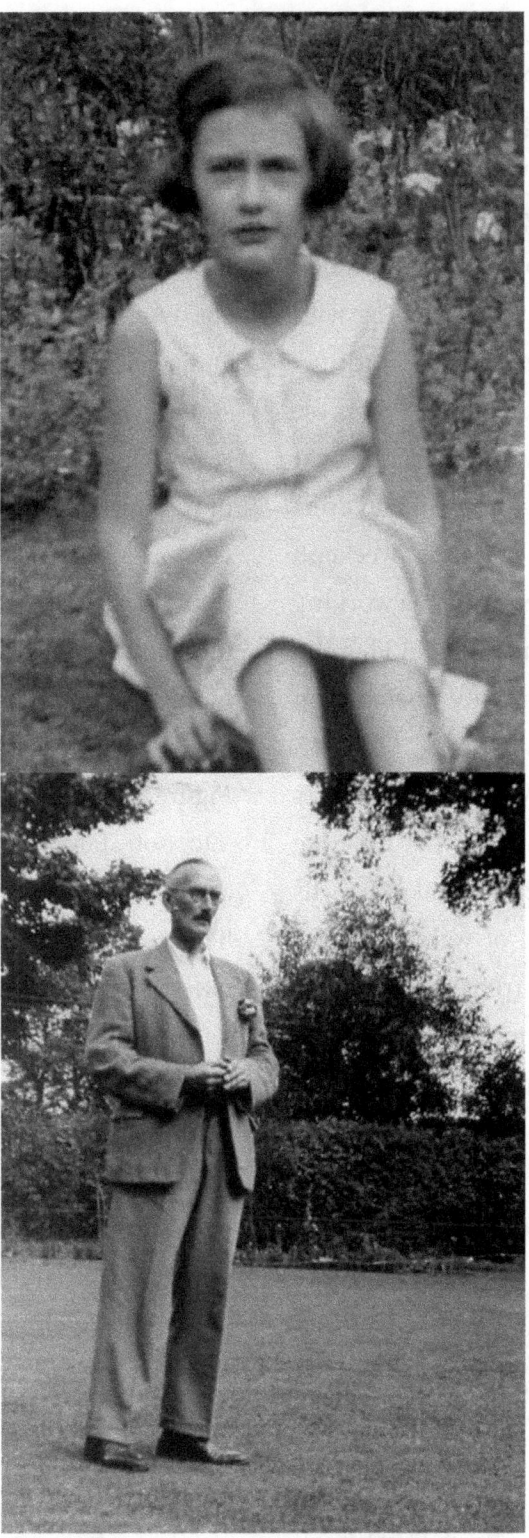

Figure 86. Daphne and her father on the lawn at 'Raycroft' in Lacock during their visit in 1936

when we went home, 'I didn't think they would like me getting blood on the school'.

The first and only time I had my father all to myself was a weekend visit in 1936 to my godmother, Mrs. Fleming, in Lacock.[2] They only had two tiny spare rooms so we couldn't all go. We drove down, my ears ringing with all the instructions given me while I dutifully watched my mother pack a case. 'Put these clean clothes on tomorrow and these the next day; bathe yourself; clean your teeth and don't forget'. It must have been a long weekend because we walked up a steep hill to a working mill one day; my father and Colonel Fleming made me a little flat boat and we floated it on a stream. (See Figures 85 and 86.)

One day, we went to Wookey Hole caves and I could hold his hand (on his false leg side the whole time instead of taking turns as his other hand was full of walking stick.) I scooped up two pebbles from the floor and took them home to our mother and Sheila as souvenirs (Woodie must have left by that time.)

Looking out of my bedroom window, I could see down into the yard at the back, across which were the stables where the Fleming's daughter, Valentine, kept three horses on which she gave riding lessons to local children. She was a very retiring person because she had a badly disfigured face. There are no descendents of the Flemings, so I won't hurt anyone by giving the reason! Before she was born, Colonel Fleming had been in India on an unaccompanied posting and, as so many did, had taken an Indian 'concubine' from whom he had picked up the worst sort of venereal disease. When he came home, they conceived Valentine and, nine months later, poor Mrs. Fleming gave birth to Valentine, totally unprepared for the shock of being handed her baby and seeing the poor little face with its 'pushed in' mouth and jaw. (See Figure 88.) Obviously, I had been well primed: 'Do not stare, do not mention anything or ask questions'. So I kept my face down in her presence, but, oh joy, she let me ride the oldest (30 years old?) horse, Goblin, because he was black, and I thought both Goblin and Valentine were the best things I had come across in my whole life. Valentine also kept rabbits in hutches in a large shed or barn and, when the war started, she bred even more rabbits for fur and meat.

I don't remember the drive down to Lacock, but the drive back to Leamington I shall never forget, sitting in the front seat next to my father, seeing the side of his face so close and singing the song he taught me as we went along. The song had about eight verses, and when we were home and triumphantly telling

---

2 Daphne's godmother, Isabella Emmeline Fleming (née Brock, 1864-1953), was born in East Burgholt, Suffolk, the daughter of Frederic Brock, Capt. of the 23rd Fusiliers, and raised in Lexden, Essex. She was married to Col. Henry Slane Fleming who died at Lacock on 2 April 1942 at the age of 85. Together they had one daughter, Valentine Emmeline Fleming, who was born in Colchester in 1898 and died (unmarried) in Bath in 1972. Col. Fleming, of the 1st Essex Regiment, was born in Tasmania, the son of Sir Valentine Fleming, Chief Justice of Tasmania. He served in the Nile Campaign and was Commandant in West Australia for three years. See *The Mercury*, Hobart, Tasmania, 15 June 1942.

Figure 87. This photograph of Daphne's father, Edward Kelly, taken in 1936, was how she best liked to remember him

Figure 88. Daphne with Mrs Fleming and Valentine at Lacock in 1951

my mother I had been good all the time and not sick – I didn't even feel sick! – I performed the song for her. She then expressed the wish that my father had taught me something more worthwhile… but as long as I didn't sing the song in public….:

'Come all you jolly jokers and listen while I hum,
The story I will tell to you of the great American bum:
They sleep in the dirt and wear a shirt
That is dirty and full of crumbs'.[3]

Alas, I can remember no more but, after being told that 'bum' meant tramp or wanderer in America and not the unmentionable bit of anatomy that it did in England, I learnt all about jumping on and off the railroad 'cars' and travelling around and having no home, all of which was thought stimulating and as good as a storybook – better because it was real.

We must all have visited the Flemings at other times as well, because it was Mrs. Fleming who told my mother the reason for poor Valentine's unusual appearance, and adding the wise advice: 'Avoid unaccompanied postings even if you have to leave the children in England'. … I suppose it is a good thing that we can't see into the future; it might be unbearably bleak or, of course, joyously wonderful.

---

3   A version of 'The Great American Bum' (or sometimes just, 'The Bum Song'), a traditional American folk song from c.1930s. A 'bum', often called a 'hobo' in America, was a vagrant, or homeless person – usually a single man – who was typically on the move, often riding the rails. They were an important feature of the depression-era 1930s American life, but remained part of the nation's fabric until at least the 1960s.

Chapter Nine

1938-1939:
Rumours of War – and York

Towards the end of the double posting at Warwick, we waited anxiously to know where we would be living next. China, that faraway place of homely memories, had been invaded by the Japanese and various parts of the world seemed to be causing our parents anxiety. Visiting adults talked seriously to each other, exuding that special adults-only atmosphere which we were not to interrupt. I think it must have been the Munich crisis that caused delays in the reshuffling of postings and various orders, counter-orders and rumours. I think it was with quite short notice that we eventually knew York was to be our next hometown, and finally everything disappeared into a removals van – except the too-small tricycles which were given away.

Our mother was a non-driver and non-cyclist, too. She said she had ridden a horse so much and was used to them balancing themselves! Oncoming traffic seemed to have a magnetic attraction for her, too! So, our father drove us up to York where we were booked into a hotel for one night and we were to have supper with our parents as a treat in the hotel, but I felt too ill by the time we got there and just went to bed. Next morning, we moved into 4, Severus Avenue, in Acomb, just on the outskirts of York. (When we and Charles, on holiday in 1990, found it, almost all the garden which was at the side of the house had been built over with a bungalow. In the photo we took then, the bungalow owner is coming out of her gate.) (See Figure 90.)

Sheila and I shared the bow-fronted room at the front. We had to use it as a playroom, as well. Our parents had the slightly smaller room (check curtain in the photo). The rest of the house was smaller than Leamington as well, but somehow the furniture, which was on the large side, was fitted in and we settled in for the next three years.

After looking at all the reachable schools, our parents decided the only possible one was the R.C. convent in York. They visited it first and made it very clear to the nuns that the very slightest hint of anyone trying to convert us and we would be removed immediately! We could catch a bus just round the corner from Severus Avenue and, after being escorted there several times, we were thought old enough and sensible enough to travel on our own.

We got to know the shopping part of York before we started at the convent, because we went shopping with our mother. I can only remember the grocer's shop; the owner was memorable because he seemed to be a walking, talking army list. As soon as our mother gave our name and address, he said, (not the exact words, but the content) …. 'Oh, Major Kelly, just moved up from Leamington, R.A.P.C, used to be Essex wasn't he…?' We were quite suspicious, when the war started, that he was actually an enemy spy. Who knows? I remember him because of that and because when we went to school on the bus, we watched for the shop and, once past, we got out at the next stop. We took turns to sit next to the window and, on one awful day, sitting next to the window, I was daydreaming and wondering why the bus was fuller that day, people even standing in the aisle when, to my horror, there was Sheila on the pavement making faces at me and waving to attract my attention. Horrors, I leapt up and squeezed my way towards the door and was first out at the next stop, luckily not far and ran back to a very cross sister. She was so practical and sensible that she never got lost in daydreams. I said there was no need to tell our mother, but she did!

The Leamington school had been quiet and everyone well-behaved, but the convent was extraordinary – everyone seemed to tiptoe and speak in whispers. Once, a nun leaned over me and said, 'You are very thin, my dear, does your mother give you plenty of rice puddings at home?' I was as indignant as our mother was when I told her! I was rather remarkably thin then, unlike Sheila who was plump, but I was stronger – they used to call it 'wiry'. When the rest of the school went to prayers after the first lesson, Sheila and I sat outside the chapel with books to read. We did spend some time listening at the door and peering through the keyhole, trying to see whatever ghastly heathen rites they were performing, but it wasn't anything remarkable or exciting so we quickly returned to the books.

Wars and rumours of wars. China had been invaded by Japan. One day, after church, we were all in the sitting room listening to the radio and our mother got up suddenly

Figure 89. This peaceful scene makes a fitting interlude between the happy family times and the turbulence ahead. It was painted by Edward Kelly near Warwick in 1937. The little girl in the doorway was posed there and Daphne (in pink) was told to sit on the left.

Figure 90. Severus Avenue, Acomb, York in 1990

with tears in her eyes and hurried out to the kitchen. 'What's the matter with Mummy?' 'Thinking about the last war, it's only about twenty years ago, you know'. I thought, twenty years, that's ages'; can one even remember what happened twenty years ago? How old does one have to be to understand fully that the loss of people you love never really leaves one? You eventually accept it, and knowing we shall all be reunited in heaven helps, but the ache is still there. By that time, we knew our mother had been married before. It was while we were in Leamington that I had a very fierce argument with a little girl at school. Somehow we were talking about grandparents and I said I had three pairs: my mother's parents in Canada (but both dead), my Kelly grandmother and my 'Grampie' and 'Grannie' Birkett. She thought I was silly because no one could have three lots of grandparents, one pair was your mother's parents and one was your father's, so I couldn't have a third pair. I said I certainly did and she was the silly one. But, when we went home, I asked our mother who the Birketts were, that we loved so much and who loved us? Up till then, she had always referred to Harold as 'Grannie Birkett's big boy', and I can't remember when she told us she had been married to him.

Figure 91. There is no date for this picture of Sheila and Daphne, but must be about this time, or a little before

Children are very sensitive to atmosphere. One had the feeling that none of the Kellys' in-laws were quite good enough for the children they had married; on the other hand, joy radiated from the Birketts. Uncle Norman was the only Birkett to have children – John, Caryll and Jerry – but they were coffee-planting in Kenya when we were small. I think all three had been born out there. When we went to Chislehurst, we were loved, we were family; sitting on the floor in the drawing room playing with the tiny brass kitchen miniatures Aunt Elsie had brought home from Burma; helping 'Grampie' stick pictures into scrapbooks for the children in the local hospital; trying to help him with crosswords; brushing the crumbs off the breakfast table and putting them on the bird table; and going for walks on the common. He used a walking stick too, only because he was getting a 'little old' (as Alasdair said to me years later!).

He made the walks very interesting, talking about the birds we saw and the flowers and letting us run ahead and stop and wait till he caught up, and then running again. If we walked the whole length of the common, we must have passed the war memorial that he had raised the funds for after World War I and organised the building of it, as the towns and villages did. Harold's name is on the memorial – did 'Grampie' wonder what we would have been like if we had been his son's children?

Aunt Elsie and Auntie Mary were the same (See Figures 93 and 94.), so years and years later, it was completely natural for Aunt Elsie and me to put our arms round each other in her garden and say 'You are my darling' to each other. I said then, 'If you ever feel you don't want to be alone, tell me and I will come'. And she did; those two weeks before she died and I went to her home at Laburnum Cottage, Dunton Green, Sevenoaks, Kent, and you did your A and O level exams, coped with the goat and chickens and the little ones.[1] I'll write a bit more about that later I hope!

Back to the time in York. One memory is of being taken on a drive in the evening for a treat. It seemed a long one, but eventually our father said, 'Oh, we are quite near the Leeds Tattoo, let's go closer and see what we can see', and soon we were going into the car park and it wasn't till we got out of the car and he took tickets from his pocket that we realised we were actually going to see the Tattoo. Open air and cool, but wonderful. We had a picnic on the moors one day, but the flies drove us mad! We were also taken round the Minster, but thought to be too young to be taken down into the crypt; instead, we were promised we would go there sometime before the end of our time in York.

Figure 92. War Memorial, Chislehurst, Kent (Remembrance Day, 2014)

All too soon, the false hopes of 'peace in our time' began to fade. Adult friends and our parents started those serious talks that we were not allowed to interrupt. Sheila and I would sit behind the sofa or chairs, occupying ourselves quietly and trying to make sense of the adults' conversations. We wished they wouldn't try to shield us from everything that wasn't sweetness-and-light and easy! We wanted to know the real world. It encroached all too soon!

Postings were changed around and our father was told he would probably be sent

---

1   Elsie Winifred Agnes Birkett died on 31 May 1978. See *The London Gazette*, 28 September 1978.

on an unaccompanied tour, so our mother laid out and packed (as far as possible) all his clothes and things he would want to take. I saw her face as she folded them lovingly and tidily, keeping all the laundry up-to-date and putting his things straight back in the trunk ready for his departure at short notice. Then it was all cancelled, so they unpacked and put the trunks away and we went out for a picnic one day to relax and be happy together. When we came home, Sheila and I found a scrap of paper behind the front door from one of the office staff, telling our father to phone for instructions; he was to go to Palestine in three days!

The next day, our father paid a flying visit to Bedford by train to say goodbye to his mother and to rent a little house for us, as we didn't want to stay in York where we had yet to make friends. He came back the next day, exhausted, and said he hadn't had time to look at the house he had rented – he knew the road and those around about from his boyhood and it was a pleasant district. Our mother had repacked the trunks, he packed all his carpentry tools except a small hammer, a screwdriver and one or two things he thought we might want. (In the three months we had been in York, he had started making cabinets for his record collection using the shed in the garden, boiling up the glue which I am glad no one uses now; it had a distinctive smell to say the least! He considered letting us try our hands at French polishing, but decided we were not quite old enough.) Sheila and I probably retired to our 'camp' under the gooseberry bushes to be miserable!

It was quite a large garden with all sorts of bushes, and lilac trees and the fruit beds. Where the woman was coming out of her bungalow in the photo (See Figure 90.), there used to be a wooden side fence with the fruit and vegetable beds just inside. There was grass behind the back of the house and, having read 'Cracker Jack the Whipman' in a comic, I spent a lot of time there with a very long length of string on a stick handle, a cork tied to the other end 'catching' upright sticks, tree branches and occasionally, when I wanted a moving target, Sheila – which made her very cross! She had a game set up on the lawn – a tennis ball on elastic hanging horizontally between two posts. We played against each other often.

One day, our father said a general was visiting the office next day and, as his ADC (Aide-de-Camp) was a friend, our father said he would invite him to lunch. The ADC said he would have come with pleasure, but had already been invited out by someone else; the general, however, who was well known to be irascible and 'difficult', had not been invited anywhere; consequently, the ADC had thought he would have to take him to a hotel. So, instead, my father invited the general to our house, and our mother went into high gear in the kitchen. Horrors, the general arrived before our father, and our mother said Sheila

Figure 93. Auntie Mary in 1949

Figure 94. Aunt Elsie in 1946

Figure 95. Strangely, no mention has been made of both Sheila and Daphne getting whooping cough and going to Weston-super-Mare, where these pictures were taken in 1938. In those days, the smell of sea air, mud and the fumes from the gas-works, were considered beneficial for whooping cough! (CMFR)

and I were to show him round the garden for a few minutes till our father came back. Showing him around the garden didn't take long and then we sat in a tiny summerhouse and looked at the garden while we tried to make suitable conversation rather overcome by his splendid uniform, red tabs and all.

Then he asked what the tennis game was and how did we play it and could he try it? Our mother said she looked out of the kitchen window and saw him, coached by us, whacking the tennis ball. Still, he looked happy and just then our father came home. The general said he hadn't had such fun for a long time and the lunch went well. Next day, while we were at school, there was a coffee party for the wives to meet the general's wife who, being introduced to our mother, said how pleased she was to meet the mother of the delightful children who thought her husband was not in the least bit 'sergeanty'. That was me who thought that all sergeants must be terrifying men and had not been able to think of a better word to describe the general to our parents. 'He wasn't at all sergeanty and he asked to play the tennis game'. Our father had repeated this to the ADC who told someone else and word got round. Our mother was very embarrassed, but the general's wife thought it was lovely and told all the other wives. It may have done the general's reputation quite a lot of good! He was human after all.

Chapter Ten

c.1939-c.1945:
Separation, Bedford and World War II

Back to unaccompanied posting…! The next day, we three saw our father off at the station at York. (See Figure 96.) As the train went off, our mother was saying, 'Keep waving, keep smiling, don't let him see you are crying'. Why not? I ask myself now, but a stiff upper lip was the fashion in those days and we were well trained. Back at the house, she sat down and we stood beside her, wondering what to do as she looked as though she was going to cry herself. Then she said, 'Snow White' is on at the cinema and if we walk quickly we will just be in time – it is better to do something than sit and mope, and if we cry in the sad bits, no one will see us'. So that is what we did.

In no time at all, a man from a garage collected the car to sell it, the removals firm that had taken our things up to York was booked to take it all down to Bedford, and we left the convent and came down to Bedford by train. We stayed one night at 56, Kimbolton Road with Granny Kelly, and the next morning walked the few roads round to 14, Richmond Road, arriving a few minutes before 8 a.m. when the van should arrive. (See Figure 97.) The house was 'rundown' on the outside and going into the tiny front hall gave the impression of total gloom! We looked into the front room – it had not been cleaned by anyone for a long time – then into the next room, just as horrible, though it had French doors onto a tiled path. There was vegetation right across the window. The indoor passage widened, as the part under the stairs had not been made into a cupboard. Another door on the left went into a tiny pantry … we eventually called it 'the shoe cleaning hole', which, describes it fairly well. A door facing us went into a 'kitchen' with a wooden dresser and an old stove for heating the water. Straight through that was an even darker room, the scullery. Both were totally dark as forsythia had grown across the tiled back path to touch the house – much worse than the bamboos in the Westbury front garden when we first came that Elizabeth disliked so much because they rustled loudly under the 'The Littles' bedroom window! The scullery beside it contained an ancient gas cooker and a copper for boiling washing and, beside it, an ancient sink which, almost unbelievably, had a pump on its right-hand side. We tried it energetically but no water came out, only from the two taps over the sink. We learned later that all the houses had had their own pumps, but they had been disconnected years before. Off the scullery was a larder with a damp back wall, and an empty but dusty coal hole.

Round the back of the house was an outside toilet which took the last third of the scullery wall. Some house owners had had a door put into their scullery walls and the toilet turned round to go against the then blocked-up back wall. As we were renting the house for only two years, we never had anything structural done, but a 'little man' was paid to build a wooden draining board over the old copper to the edge of the sink, to put boards across the front of the coal hole before we had coal delivered and a few bookshelves in the dining room. Coke (or anthracite) for the kitchen stove was dumped around the back of the house, and eventually we had that corner boarded off to keep the fuel from spreading out across any of the tiny grass plot with beds round three sides.

On that moving-in morning, the whole place gave the impression of decay and gloom. Still the van was missing. Our mother said, 'If I just had some rags or a brush, we could start cleaning', and then she sat on the bare wooden stairs and started to cry. Like a Greek chorus, we hovered beside her saying, 'It's only for two years till Daddy comes'. … Little did we know - sixteen years for me till I married Daddy and longer for our mother and Sheila! Mummie died when Charles was nine months old,[1] and Sheila stayed on in the house for a while, but moved to a downstairs flat in St. George's Road till she went to Canada. At the start of the war, all rents were fixed to prevent racketeering, and £50 annually was what we paid all through the war, and for a while afterwards.

Eventually, the furniture van arrived and everything was brought in. The wife from next door on our attached side appeared with a tray of mugs, teapot and milk and biscuits, having counted up the removals men and us. I can't remember when we had the stairs carpeted, but it must have been soon. The beautiful blue Chinese carpet went into the sitting room, but had to have one corner turned under where

[1] Muriel Kelly died in Bedford on 13 October 1957. Charles was born on 8 April 1957.

Chapter Ten ~ c.1939-c.1945: Separation, Bedford and World War II

Figure 96. York Rail Station, where Edward Kelly departed for war duty in Palestine, 1939

Figure 97. 14 Richmond Road, Bedford (the house on the left), n.d.

Figure 98. Mother and the Girls in the garden of 14 Richmond Road, soon after moving in.

Figure 99. St Andrew's Church, Bedford, 1932

Figure 100. St. Andrew's School, 78 Kimbolton Road, Bedford

Figure 101. Below: Sheila and Daphne at St Andrew's School in 1939

it was partially hidden by the piano. Its two companion rugs neatly carpeted the tiny hall where there was just room for the best Chinese carved box; if one squeezed past it and turned sharp left, there was the sitting room, which almost 'disappeared' under the large sofa, the two matching chairs, the brass side tables, as well as the piano!

When we had our adult cycles, we had to come in the front door, manoeuvre them *carefully* past the Chinese chest and the newel post at the bottom of the stairs and into their back-wheel racks under the stairs, where the school macs and blazers hung. Outdoor shoes also lived there.

Our father's roll-top desk, the dining room table and chairs, and a tiny side table more than filled the second room; the plain black Chinese chest and a wooden kitchen table went into the 'kitchen' and we used to do our work there as it was warm. China and glasses were kept in the kitchen but the cooking was done in the 'scullery' with a tiny folding table between the cooker and the draining board to put the used tableware and cooking things on before washing up. Another kitchen table against the side wall completed the kitchen – no 'fitments', no fridge, though Sheila did get one sometime after I had left home.

Upstairs, there was a bathroom, three bedrooms and a tiny room where we put all the empty crates and boxes – only for two years ….! For my O-level birthday present, our mother somehow restacked the crates to clear the top of a table (it had been our father's painting table in Leamington), made room for a chair and emulsioned the visible bits of wall and it became my 'study': I did all my homework there – no heat in winter – but solitary, uninterrupted, fast-reading time: bliss. We had two single beds in the front room, and the one behind it was the spare room with a double bed. Our mother preferred the room at the back of the house because it looked onto the tiny garden, and the evening sun came in.

Our grandmother wanted us to go to St. Peter's Church, which she had been attending for some time, having taken a dislike to the previous vicar of St. Andrew's. Instead, we went to St. Andrew's up Kimbolton Road. (See Figure 99.) The vicar then lived in a dark house in Pembroke Road (or Avenue) and it was there we went to our pre-confirmation lessons. The vicarage was built on the church plot, a large triangle, quite soon after I think. St. Peter's was 'low' church, St. Andrew's was 'high'; the vicar, Mr. Down, gave an occasional sermon explaining the meanings of the ceremonies and which meant that there was plenty of movement amongst the servers and clergy and plenty for children to watch, as Mr. Down said. Our mother, who was shy, could never bring herself to take us up to the front pews where we might have seen even more, so we sat in the fourth from the back on the right side every Sunday. Quite near the back door in case either of us felt sick or faint, which occasionally we did at the early service which was long, and we never ate or drank before going to that service.

When she knew we were coming to Bedford, our grandmother lost no time in going up Kimbolton Road from '56' and visiting the two sisters who ran a school for young ladies. Our father's cousin (Bertram's sister) had gone to that school after their parents died and she spent most of the holidays with either Granny Kelly or our father's sister, Auntie Kathleen (Michael and Jennifer's mother) and Uncle Lennie, though I think they were living in London then. Our parents had decided, as much as they could in the one weekend in York, that we would go to the Bedford High School, and I remember our mother's indignation that Granny Kelly should presume to make arrangements for anything without consulting us. Granny Kelly said, 'It is what Edward would want' which it wasn't, but for the sake of family harmony ('and it is only for two years'), we went to St. Andrew's School. (See Figures 100 and 101.) The headmistress didn't teach but she took the daily prayers (and hymns). Her younger sister, known as 'Miss Kathleen', did teach and there were two other teachers; no more I think, unless someone different took the hockey lessons for which we had to walk up to the park, wearing the most ghastly light-blue stockings. It was definitely, then, a small private 'dame' school.[2]

It was somewhere in Bedford that we all went to be measured and fitted and issued with gas masks, and soon after everyone had to make second visits to have an extra filter taped onto the end as the Germans had invented a new gas which would go through the original filters. We were also issued with cardboard boxes to keep the masks in; most families, however, invested in canvas covers because the boxes alone would have soon worn out as they had to be carried about at all times, and at school they were hung on the back of each pupil's chair. We had practices at school and at home, timed to be done in a few seconds – put down everything else, open case, chin in first, put on mask and breathe normally. When we practised at home we used to tell our mother she should practise too, but she always thought of something she had to do in the kitchen or somewhere, so she would put her mask on and bolt out of the room. It wasn't for quite a while afterwards that our Uncle Norman Birkett came to stay with us on one of his 'leaves', that she confessed to him that she felt so claustrophobic when she put her's on, that she had to get out of the room so she could take some air in through the side of the mask, which one could do by pushing a couple of fingers under the rubber side pieces. Uncle Norman persuaded her to put her mask on and they sat on the sofa together, and he held her hand to stop her panicking till she had proved to herself that she could really breathe.

---

2 St. Andrew's School was founded in 1896 as a school for the daughters of gentlemen. Today, it is an independent school for girls, aged 3-16, and boys aged 3-9.

Sheila and I walked together to St. Andrew's, and then again home. One of our mother's worries was that if the sirens went and bombs did drop, we might be *en route* to school. I think she timed us when we left home, so that if the sirens did go before we could have been at school, she could be out like a shot to search for us if a bomb dropped nearby. (Everyone was issued with an identity number and, I think, a mass-produced 'bracelet'. Most of us bought a silver bracelet with the number on it.) We were told that if the siren went, we were to go on to school if we were more than halfway there. If a plane flew over before the all clear, we were to take shelter in the front porch of the nearest house. The sirens frequently went off, but few bombs were dropped. The German planes flew over (or near) Bedford on their way to more important targets, Coventry included. Sometimes, damaged German planes turned back before they had dropped their loads and they would jettison them anywhere *en route*. Probably the one that dropped on the allotments a couple of roads away from us was

Figure 102. Edward Kelly occasionally sent little paintings back to the family; this one is of Jerusalem, n.d.

thrown out for that reason.

Our own air raid precautions had consisted of having wooden doors built to go outside the dining room French doors. The dining room was considered the best room to make into one's shelter as escape was possible through the French doors if the rest of the house fell down and blocked the door into the front passage/hall. At first, if the sirens went in the night, we all went downstairs and sat in the dining room, ready to duck under the table if bombs started to land around us. I think our pussy had the safest place as we kept her bed, which was a wooden box with a cushion in it, in the kneehole of our father's roll top desk. I think it was that bomb on the allotments that blew the wooden shutters open and rattled the French doors rather excitingly, and we all went under the table. When we came out, our mother was very indignant that the blast had rent her nightie all down one side! She always maintained that it wouldn't otherwise have torn, as she went under the table only because it was her best and very good nightie!

The only other bomb of much personal 'interest' to us appeared much later in the war, when we were going to the High School. We were meant to cycle close to each other, and, of course, in single file, but for some reason I was being infuriatingly slow and Sheila said she wasn't going to be late because of me. So she started without me. That didn't worry me because I cycled faster than her. I was halfway to school when the sirens went, wailing up and down, so I speeded up a bit, expecting to catch her up, but she must have put on a spurt for she was almost at the gates when a very noisy bomb fell from the sky. Pushing her cycle through the gate and into her cycle stand, she heard a rustle in a tree beside her and a chunk of metal landed quite near to her. She hurried on as the in-going bell was just ringing (or whatever they did, I can't remember!). I arrived seconds later and bolted through the entrance door, fast, not because of bombs but because I really had cut it fine that day. One teacher must have been even later as she passed the piece of metal which she picked up and took to show the other teachers, declaring it was still warm. Apparently, a lot of 'warm' metal landed in and around Bedford on that occasion, as the bomb had gone smack into the middle of the salvaged metal dump. (Our little front gate and the railing along the brick wall were probably on the dump! We had sacrificed them at the beginning of the war and had a flimsy wooden-slat gate and top to the wall put up instead. Sheila and I painted it and, every now and then, repainted it over the years.)

Figure 103. Daphne at the bottom of the Richmond Road garden

Figure 104. Mother's portrait taken in Bedford in 1939, probably for her identity card

Chapter Eleven

c.1939-c.1945: Evacuees

Back at the start of the war, a large number of evacuees arrived in Bedford, and our mother went down to the hall where they were temporarily accommodated. Despite telling the authorities that we only had one double bed spare, we were allocated two large teenagers from a secondary school in the East End of London. They were 'delivered' to us later that day – two seventeen-year-old boys, Lionel and David. Our mother had bought a piece of ham (without the help of their ration books): I suppose she felt that it could be 'spun out' and shared equally while we got to know their appetites and maybe they would have food provided in their temporary school accommodation. David followed her to the kitchen and announced he was a Jew and he didn't eat ham, etc., etc. Our mother rightly said he should have been sent to a Jewish household then!

After supper, they asked her for a front door key as they wanted to go out and see where all their friends were and might be late back. Our mother replied that they had been sent to us as schoolboys and, as such, they were not allowed to stay out late. I don't remember if they did go out that night, but that evening the sirens went and the five of us went into the dining room. I was surprised when our mother asked Lionel to come out of his corner and check if the French doors were properly closed. She said later that, as Lionel was firmly seated in the safest corner and was shaking violently and looking on the verge of panicking, she thought he would feel better if he moved about. Then we chatted and she said surely they were rather old to be evacuated as they would be leaving school at the end of the term or year and joining up. Both said, oh no, their fathers knew how to get them into 'reserved' work or some safe place and work. The next day she went to the evacuation authorities and said she did not want two huge young men with us while we had no man of ours at home. They were with us three days and then moved to the home of Bedford's chief warden, I think in De Parys Avenue. There they stayed for quite a time, refusing to lift a finger on their Sabbath, even to switch on a light, and Lionel continued to hide and shake through all air raid sirens. They were also in trouble for staying out much too late doing things unspecified to our tender and probably over-protected ears.

Their replacements, from a totally unsuitable house in Bedford, were two seven-year-olds, Albert and Freddie. They were brought round to us later that day. Albert was bright and, because he had often worked with his father at weekends and holidays pushing the costermonger's[1] barrow round the East End of London, he could do mental arithmetic faster than one could imagine. Freddie was thin, dirty to the point of smelling, dressed in a vest and disgusting shorts held up by thin braces of perished elastic with metal clips that scratched his back, and plimsolls that were so small that he had trodden down the back to make room for his heels.

[1] A street seller of fruit and vegetables from a handcart.

When his little cardboard suitcase was opened for clean clothes and, hopefully, pyjamas, ('What are pyjamas?' said both), it was empty except for a half-full bottle of tomato ketchup. Freddie spoke so little and so badly that we had to get Albert, who knew him from school in London, to translate. The first evening, we showed them the tiny back garden and said that was where we played, definitely not the roads or pavements. Then our mother asked Freddie to latch the back gate for us. (I think she had secretly unlatched it just before.) She spoke slowly and carefully and eventually he understood and went along the path and pushed the latch into place. When she thanked him, he looked amazed: it was probably the first time anyone had thanked him for anything! Thus we knew that he could understand and therefore learn.

Albert could read and write. Freddie couldn't do more than make two-year-old scribbles on paper. Albert said he didn't often come to school. Later we asked him where he ate his tea, but all we could understand was that it was on a doorstep, half a mile from home. Albert's father visited us one weekend to see if his son was alright, and he brought with him all the overripe fruit from his barrow. His mother also came once with a suitcase of clothes for Albert and quite a lot more for Freddie. She said she did pass on clothes to Freddie's mother sometimes but didn't often see them on Freddie, whose mother had some menial work somewhere in the East End and,

I think, was illiterate and not very bright; no father for Freddie.

During the first night with us, poor Freddie wet the double bed, for which we were not prepared, so our mother spent that day washing and somehow drying the mattress. The evening before, she had washed Freddie's disgusting shorts and got those dry so that she could walk them down the road opposite Goldington Avenue, where they went to school. She went on to town and somewhere managed to buy enough clothes and a pair of shoes for him to have a complete change while one set was being washed. I guess she also bought a waterproof sheet for the bed. I know she put a potty under the bed and explained about using it, and I think he did.

On Saturdays, we used to play schools and both little boys seemed to think it was fun. I concentrated on Freddie who soon blossomed into a sweet little boy, and very soon learned to speak so we could understand what he was saying as he began to chat. Albert had one ambition. Our mother had had white hair since 1917, within a year of Harold's death, but she was young enough to be our mother, so Albert just couldn't work out how old she might be. He tried time and time again, asking oblique questions – and more straightforward ones such as what year were we born in, and adding 'and you'. 'I've forgotten - it is so long ago', she would reply.

Occasionally, when we didn't play 'schools', we played 'families' and with dolls and bears for extra 'children'. We took turns to get up in the mornings and get to school, and have meals at home, and pretend to cook and so on. 'Getting rid of nits from hair' was not a game! Most of the evacuees had nits. The health visitor also prescribed ointment for the sores on Freddie's shoulders. There was a small allowance given for each evacuee, but it barely covered their food, certainly not complete sets of clothes. Also, the time and energy expended on them really drained our mother, till she felt so tired and worn that she went to see our doctor and he gave her a letter saying she was not well enough to look after evacuees. The boys were then found a home on the other side of Goldington Road, nearer their school, but a tiny house and, I think, no other children. Albert's parents wrote and begged us to keep them because they were so happy; their school teacher expressed her gratitude for the way Freddie had blossomed, talked and could now read and write – not a lot – but enough for him to get on at school, which he now seemed to enjoy.

We introduced them to toothpaste and toothbrushes while they were with us. I hope they kept that habit even if they couldn't afford toothpaste! Those times when they visited us, they begged us to have them back because there were no other children in their present house and there were no napkins or napkin rings! They had been mystified by ours but, when their use was explained, they thought it was fun. Learning to fold his napkin and get it into the ring was one of the first skills that Freddie learned. Any words of encouragement brought a glow of pleasure to his bony little face that had initially been quite blank.

We had them only for three months, or a little longer. They walked up to visit us a couple of times, but I think, like so many evacuees when they found London wasn't being flattened by bombs, they went back home. If they survived the war, I'm sure Albert grew up to be a successful businessman and I hope he inherited his parents' kindness. Did Freddie go back to having his tea on a doorstep half a mile from home, or was he able to build on the little bit of education and affection he had while he was in Bedford, and have a happier life? I do hope when we get to heaven we shall know.

Chapter Twelve

c.1939-c.1945:
Bedford High School and Wartime Life

School at St. Andrew's became increasingly boring and petty; it definitely didn't 'stretch' us. Sheila continued to get on well with maths. In Leamington, if either of us had a problem with maths homework, our father would explain it to Sheila, as she picked it up easily. I just couldn't understand maths, and the more I felt frustrated and the more my father wondered how anyone could be so dense, I suppose I just gave up. My mother could explain basic arithmetic so that I could understand. She always started off, 'Well, I didn't have as good an education as Daddy, but we used to do it this way…', and it made sense. However, when we got past straight arithmetic to fractions and theorems and pointless things like log tables, I was lost. History, geography and English and 'Scripture' I loved, but there wasn't enough of that at St. Andrew's. Some years later, when Miss Bell and Miss Kathleen retired and a new headmistress arrived at St. Andrew's, the number of pupils went up and the curriculum improved. (Our cousin Apphia went there, eventually; James went to Bedford School.) So we applied to the High School and were accepted. (See Figure 105.) To get there every day, we would have to cycle through the town and, on games afternoons (we came home for lunch), we would cycle past the school and another mile or so toward Bromham to the playing fields. (When we had first bought the cycles, we wheeled them home and, after that, we wheeled them up to the park and learned to ride on the paths there.)

The sirens continued to wail often, but nothing really damaging was dropped. It was

Figure 105. Bedford High School. Founded in 1882

Figure 106. A picture taken around 1946, of Sheila and Daphne with James and Apphia Kelly (cousins)

usually at night that the sirens went off and, eventually, like most people, we stayed in bed where at least it was warm until the all-clear – one long sustained note – and we could sink back into sleep. At some point, the neighbours next door moved, and the empty house was used to re-house a family, the Keens, who had had their home and business premises obliterated when Coventry was bombed.[1] Mr. Keens started up his business (or was helped to start it) as he made small electrical things which were essential for something, round in the brick 'shed' in the next road.

The shed stretched half across the Keens' back garden, the whole way across ours and half across the next garden. They had two children – a girl about nineteen and a son who was seventeen. When he got to call-up age, he was chosen (by ballot) to be a Bevan boy, that is, to be a coal miner, which upset his mother a lot because she wanted him to have a white collar job eventually and thought a time in one of the services would have been a good start.

She was a kind, straightforward woman and she and our mother had lots of chats across the back-garden wall. Our scullery walls were not soundproof if one bumped a table near the mutual wall, so eventually, if one had a bit of news to impart, the one would give the wall three raps, (we used the handle of our bread knife for that), and the other gave two to indicate she had heard, and then both would go into the garden. Mrs. Keens died of cancer when I was fifteen or sixteen, I think.[2] She surprised our mother by saying that she had been confirmed in her teens, though rarely in a church since, but she would like to take communion. Our vicar came, probably the next day, and our mother and I were with her. Again, she surprised us all by joining very firmly in the Lord's Prayer and then, sounding astonished, she remarked, 'There's a light, a very bright light, I see it!' The vicar said, 'Yes, there is Light'. She shut her eyes to sleep, our mother kissed her and we left. She died very soon afterwards.

Our mother's relatives in Canada used to send food parcels to us sometimes, and our mother always shared things around. For example, an extra packet of tea to Mrs. Keens because they drank a lot, or maybe to Mrs. Down, the vicar's wife, because they had so many people coming to the vicarage in need of a cheering cup of tea![3] Other treasures in short supply were given to the friends we gradually made and, of course, to Granny Kelly and to Auntie Kathleen Bulkley and her two children, Michael and Jennifer. (See Figures 107 and 108.) The last three came to live with Granny Kelly soon after the war started as they had lived in London. Uncle

---

1 Samuel and Amelia Keens of 16 Richmond Road, Bedford.

2 According to the records, Amelia Keens died on 30 October 1954. See *Index of Wills and Administration, 1858-1966*. Mr. Keens died in October 1958.

3 The wife of the Revd. Alexander Thornton Down, Vicar of St. Andrew's, Bedford, from 1938 to 1946. In 1957, after serving in Belize and then back at Bedford, Mr. Down retired to Romney Marsh, Kent. He died in April 1961. See Obituary, *Church Times*, 14 April 1961.

Lennie had a room somewhere in London as he was a sound recorder for film-making crews, and had to be near the work. For some reason, he was nicknamed Bill and it was as Bill Bulkley that he appears in the credits of his films, notably in 'Whisky Galore'.

Our Canadian Auntie Lil and Uncle Romald Helmer were really in pretty dire straits themselves.[4] (See Figure 109.) Their daughter Isabel had been ill for years, since she was about thirteen, with an obscure disease which gradually debilitated her, and their every penny was spent on treatments and medicines of any sort they hoped would help her.[5] Every year, when the corncobs were ready for harvest, Auntie Lil would sit at their kitchen table and, with a knife, strip cob after cob and dry the grains, sew them into a cotton flour bag and send them to us. (Cotton flower bags were very useful. One was enough to make a short-sleeved summer shirt. I made Sheila one and embroidered flowers round the collarless neckline!) It was the best tasting corn I have ever had and a heap of that in the centre of one's plate with a tiny share of butter on top and a sprinkle of salt would be a real treat for a supper. Auntie Lil said once (by letter of course) that our mother didn't need to worry that she was giving her sister (herself) extra work, because it was a good reason to sit down while she stripped the cobs!

Sheila and I, when we were eleven and twelve respectively, went to pre-confirmation classes at the vicarage and walked there, sometimes after dark, which was exciting in a way as (with the blackout) there were no street lights and no lights from windows. We all had black linings to our curtains and not a chink of light was allowed; wardens patrolled the streets, and knocked on doors if they saw even the tiniest crack of light, because even the lighted end of a cigarette could be seen from a plane even if miles above. One evening, Auntie Kathleen started to walk round to us, probably to share a letter or a bit of news. It was a particularly dark night and she crossed from '56' and walked straight into one of the trees that lined the road. Having a large nose, it took the full force of her usually fast walk and bled a lot,

---

[4] Some confusion surrounds the spelling of Daphne's uncle's Christian name. Officially (and apparently in common use by the family), it was 'Romald', though on numerous documents and records it appeared as 'Ronald' (or 'R.H.'). He had been born in Columba, Ceylon, in 1875, but baptized in Romaldkirk Yorkshire, later the same year. In 1899, age 24, he emigrated to Canada, where he became involved in farming. He and Aunt Lil married in 1905; nine years later, he was appointed the first Superintendent of the Summerland Experimental Farm (now the Summerland Ornamental Gardens) in British Columbia. His early work there focused on feeding trials for livestock, growing cereals, developing commercial fertilizers, the growing of hemp (later illegal), and experimenting with new varieties of fruits, vegetables and ornamental plants. Aunt Lil played a full role in this work, her hospitality being described glowingly in one account as 'well known. Whenever she heard three toots of a train whistle, which signified that a train was stopping at Winslow Siding, she would start preparing a meal for the visitors. The Helmers' personalities served as a guide to many people who followed them in forming the station's reputation.' As another source put it, 'Helmer was a very generous, openhearted person and Mrs. Helmer's hospitality was boundless.' See W. W. Fleming, *Summerland Research Station 1914-1985* (1987), 18. In June 1923, about the time Isabel became ill, Romald resigned as Superintendent at the Experimental Farm. He then took up farming at Langley, east of Vancouver. He died in 1967; Aunt Lil had died four years earlier.

[5] Edith Lilian Isabel Helmer, daughter of Uncle Romald and Aunt Lil, was born in 1910 and died, aged 39, on 1 January 1950, and was buried at Fort Langley Cemetery, British Columbia. See *British Columbia, Canada, Death Index, 1872-1990*.

Figure 107.
Auntie Kathleen and Uncle Leonard
(Lennie, or Bill) Bulkley (1950s)

Figure 108.
Michael and Jennifer Bulkley (1950s)

Figure 109. Aunt Lil (Edith Lilian Helmer, left); Isabel Helmer (third from left); Romald Helmer (second from right); Romald Helmer Jr (right, in shorts). A photo taken at the Summerland Experimental Farm, c.1925

and hurt so much she thought she must have broken it (she had). She quickly came to the conclusion that our mother would be able to help her more than her mother, so she kept walking around to us. Our mother said she got an awful shock when she opened our front door and there was Auntie Kathleen well-spattered with blood…

When London endured the worst blitz, we could see the glow of the city burning on the horizon. As the war went on and the tide turned, hundreds of bombers went from surrounding airfields on the start of their flights to Germany. Our cousin, Romald (son of Aunt Lil and Uncle Romald),[6] came to England with the Canadian Air Force. News by letter was slow then, but as soon

---

6 Romald Helmerow Helmer, Jr (b.1916).

as they had been notified, Aunt Lil wrote to our mother and told us that Romald was in hospital in Ely with a broken back. We made haste to visit him. It was a long train journey, but we made it and we were able to write to Canada with details. He was in a plaster cast from his armpits to his thighs; sitting was very difficult; he preferred to lie or stand, but we were assured he would recover and walk normally. He did eventually have an operation to strengthen his spine by taking a piece of his shin and putting it into his spine.

He came to visit us on sick-leave several times. One time, while we were at school, he lay on the sitting room floor and, with paint boxes borrowed from us, painted beautiful studies of dogs' heads and drew cartoons. (After the war, he lived on his parent's farm in Langley, British Columbia, helped with all the farm work, and drew cartoons for local and occasionally other papers to earn his living. If the family was really short of money, he would do a few shifts at the local sawmill! He had a wonderful sense of humour and was as gentle and loving a person as his parents.)

Figure 110. Daphne and Sheila, c.1939 – with a doll apparently named 'Hilary'

Coming back from that first and, I think, only visit to Ely was more exciting than we had expected. We knew the blackout would be in force when we returned, and we knew all the station names had been removed, so we had counted the stations we passed while on the way to Ely and then, on the way back, we counted again and duly got out at the same number. On the platform we looked about and nothing looked right for Bedford station, however: they had put in an extra stop and we were on Flitwick platform, twelve miles from Bedford. The train was just about moving off as we scrambled back in.

Two other young servicemen stayed with us during their leaves: both were Archers, two of the four boys who were sons of the Padre who wrote to our mother in WWI. Bill only came once but the youngest, Geoff,[7] came quite often before the Canadians went to France on the D-Day invasion. He also came several other times while on sick leave, as he was wounded when the Canadians were held up trying to get to Caen. Geoff was huge; we used to joke that he filled a doorway, in both directions. The family was in fairly dire financial straits till the boys grew up. Even so, Mrs. Archer sent us several parcels after Geoff had told her how difficult things were in England for civilians. I know it took vast quantities of food to fill him when he came to visit us! After WWI, when his father had died quite young, the wife wrote to our mother and said she thought he was just worn out by all the heartbreak and physical strain of the war. I think our mother was one of the few widows that Padre Archer kept in touch with, as he had told her during the war that her letters were so helpful to him in the middle of all that grief and horror, and he asked her then if he could quote or show bits of her letters to other widows.

---

[7] During the Second World War, Geoffrey Archer served with the 30th Light Anti-Aircraft Battery, from December 1941 until July 1944, when he received the Commendation for Gallantry in the Field from Field Marshal Montgomery in Normandy, when he was wounded. He was discharged October 1945. After returning to Canada he was ordained in the Anglican Church, enjoying a long, rich and faithful ministry. He died in Vancouver, where he and his wife Margaret had lived for many years, in 2004. At that time his brother, William, was living in Toronto. See: www.vancouver.anglican.ca/news/the-rev-geoff-archer

Chapter Thirteen

c.1945-c.1946: Hopes Dashed

All those first years in Bedford, a part of our lives seemed to be 'on hold' waiting for our father to come home – so many things were deferred to 'when Daddy comes home'. I think his posting was lengthened to three years, but, without checking a lot of papers, I can't quite remember – maybe he went to Cyprus then. He described the King David's Hotel in Jerusalem being blown up, and his post office where the bodies were taken away by the shovelful, literally.[1] Our mother didn't think he should write the awful details of this experience, but he thought we led a much too sheltered life: he was probably right, but how else could it have been for most of us then. Geographically, our life was limited by the distance we could walk, bus or, later, cycle. A great blessing was the river; when we could afford it, we three hired a punt or rowing boat and took a picnic. Our mother taught us to row and paddle; I taught myself to punt by watching other river users.

Very few families had fathers at home at that time, and those fathers who were, were mostly old or ill. Anyway, the food in Palestine was poor and our father was frequently unwell. He wrote how sometimes he saw donkeys and even camels being taken round the back of the place where he was billeted and noticed that most of them didn't come out again, and that the meat at meals was very tough and had a peculiar flavour. One morning, the post came at breakfast time and there was a letter from

---

[1] This refers to the bombing of the King David Hotel in Jerusalem on 22 July 1946, which was carried out by the militant terrorist Zionist underground organization, the Irgun. At the time, the British administrative headquarters for Palestine was housed in the hotel. Ninety-one people of various nationalities were killed and forty-six were injured in the blast.

him. Our mother started to read it while we ate, and I can remember the way she stopped, read out, 'I may be posted back fairly soon', and then stopped again and started to cry. She said she was so happy but she couldn't see the rest and we must get off to school. We went off and I was so happy I couldn't concentrate on anything, just thinking, 'He's coming home, he's coming home', and longing to get back and hear the rest of the letter. Oddly, she didn't read us the rest of the letter, just told us bits. How in love can one be? Or, was it that it was impossible to 'think the unthinkable'?

What he had written in the rest of that letter was that, when he was posted back to England, he wouldn't be coming home to us. While he was in Palestine, he had got himself entangled with the wife of another officer. (How was she out there if the postings were unaccompanied?) All women were attracted to him and he was too easily flattered. She had approached him and said she felt he was the only person who would understand what a mess her life was in and how badly her husband treated her. (She drank too much, we discovered later.) He talked to her, trying to help her and, in no time, her husband, who was probably glad to be rid of her, was citing him as co-respondent in a divorce case.[2] To be cited like that was, at that time, disgrace enough, but with the wife of a fellow officer… that was the pits of shame! He said he couldn't desert her as that would be dishonourable. Our mother wrote back and said (well, I don't know exactly what she said): didn't he think he was letting us down, behaving dishonourably to us, having ignored his friends' warnings that she (the other woman) had had affairs with other men and was in every way trouble. No wonder our mother was run-down and worn out, and probably verging on a breakdown.

Of course, the family in Bedford knew about this[3] and, after a long time, our mother told the vicar and Mrs. Down and, much later, the doctor, who was the son of the doctor who attended our father after his motorcycle accident and knew the whole family. A lot of people must have guessed that there was

---

2 On 23 November 1943, the *Darby Evening Standard* carried the following story: 'Brigadier Edric Montague Bastyan, now serving abroad, was granted a *decree nisi* in the Divorce Court today against Mrs. Marjorie Dorothy Bastyan [née Bowle] (b. March 1911), on the grounds of her misconduct with the co-respondent, Colonel Edward Rupert Kelly. There was no defence. The marriage took place in 1934. The case of Brigadier Bastyan, whose evidence was given by affidavit, was that in 1938 his wife accompanied him from Malta to Palestine, and she insisted on their living in a hotel. There was trouble between them over her extravagance. Her monthly bill for drinks and cigarettes for herself and her friends sometimes coming to more than £23. In Jerusalem, she spent a good deal of time in the company of the co-respondent. Early in 1940 he was transferred to England and from October of that year he and Mrs. Bastyan lived together in London'. No further information on Mrs. Bastyan has been uncovered. Brigadier Bastyan (1903-1980) served in various capacities as a senior officer in the British Army, including Assistant Quarter-Master General in the Middle East from 1941 to 1942, and commander of the British Forces in Hong Kong from 1957 to 1960. He continued to receive promotion, eventually becoming Lieutenant General Sir Edric Montague Bastyan, KCMG, KCVO, KBE, CB. He retired from the Army in 1960 and was then appointed Governor of South Australia (1961 to 1968) and Governor of Tasmania (1968 to 1973). He was the last non-Australian to serve in either post. In 1944, he married Victoria Eugenie Helen Bett in Rome. He may have been related to Major General Kenneth Cecil Orville Bastyan, CB, CBE (1906-1975) of Bedford. See the *Australian Dictionary of National Biography*, volume 13 (1993).

3 Though Edward Kelly's parents were both deceased at the time, his father having died in July 1930 and his mother in September 1943. Perhaps the complicated events surrounding Edward's extramarital behavior hastened her ill-health and eventual death.

Figure 111. Daphne (left) punting on the River Ouse in 1951 with her Advanced Needlework Group

something wrong because anyone who was posted to London or Leicester would have managed to get home sometimes. Our pathetic reasons for his non-appearance, such as 'Travelling is very tiring for him with a false leg, it is better for him to rest at weekends,'… I remember the evening she told us, we were fourteen and fifteen by then (1942 or 1943): she said he said he probably wouldn't come home, but that we must never give up hope and we must never feel bitter or love him any less. Also, we wouldn't discuss this with anyone so that it would make it easier for him when he *did* come home. He did pay one quick visit to his mother who was ill, and he came to us for one night, leaving the next morning early. He had got to us in time for a sort of tea mid-afternoon and no sooner were we sitting down than one of the local busybodies, who must have seen him walking to us, called and sat herself down and joined in our tea and stayed far too long, saying how nice it was to see him, etc., etc. I think we all felt like strangling her!

One other time, he was coming through Bedford *en route* for somewhere else, Sheila and I met him at the station and we had tea in a local hotel. Our mother said she couldn't bear to see him for that short time. Waiting for the train, we stood one at each end of the platform as there were two bridges over the lines. I saw him get out of the middle of the train and I ran so fast that people looked at me. He was walking away from me, but I caught up and hugged him from behind and then properly as he turned around. He felt just the same as when I had been small and shared one of the big sitting room chairs with him, leaning on him. He wrote to us all after and said it was one of the best moments in his whole life, that I still loved him…silly man.

Even then, he could have extricated himself from the mess his life was becoming. He had a flat in Leicester, and then in London when he was posted there, and he invited us to for a weekend several times. But as he said, 'of course, the woman would be there', we certainly didn't want to go. The vicar, Mr. Down, talked through with our mother the possible benefits of a legal separation rather than divorce, arguing that it was pointless to secure a divorce as the sins were already committed and a divorce would mean giving up hope that he would eventually come home. A separation would mean that he was obliged to give our mother a fair share of his income. They didn't have a joint bank account, but every month he paid into the bank a sum they had agreed before he went to Palestine. As everything became more expensive and the woman (I have almost forgotten her name and I really don't want to remember it anyway) was a big spender on everything she wanted, including drink, he would cut down on what he paid in.[4] By the time we had reached the fifth-form at the High School, that is, once we had done our O-levels (School Certificate then), he was urging us to leave school and get paid work as we should be helping to support our mother – and anyway getting out into the world was a much better education than being at school. That was some of the least hurtful things he used to write; not in every letter – so one never knew when those blue air-letters floated on to the mat, whether the contents were going to be 'alright', or yet another hurtful episode. If they arrived before school, I'm surprised I didn't get run over, given my attempts to stop crying and not look 'bleary eyed' when I got to the classroom.

At some stage, he had a posting in Cyprus: it was warm and sunny and beautiful, and he said that when he retired he would like to live in Cyprus and concentrate on his watercolour painting; he was fed up with England and the stuffy bigoted people and the horrible climate, etc. When he did retire (1946), he and the woman went to Cyprus, but it was the cold, wet, muddy season; moreover, he found wired-off

---

4 Despite his (Edward Kelly's) promotion to Lieutenant-Colonel Staff Paymaster in October 1940.

camps, full of Jews who had been intercepted trying to sail to Palestine. His living expenses had gone up too, so another cut for us. He admired the Jews for their efforts and decided to go back to Palestine/Israel and settle there, which they (he and the woman) did.

At the start of the war, as well as Auntie Kathleen, Michael and Jennifer living with Granny Kelly, Auntie Georgie and James and Apphia had come to Bedford and bought a very nice cottage just off Kimbolton Road with a footpath through into Pemberley Avenue. Uncle Arthur was abroad like so many other fathers. When he was wounded, Granny Kelly came running round to us before breakfast; when our mother had comforted her as best she could, she invited her to stay for breakfast which she enjoyed very much and ate what seemed to me a great deal of scrambled egg. I expect it was our mother's ration as we had about one egg per person a week, supplemented for cooking by powdered egg which came from the U.S.A. One could scramble powdered egg, but it had a very distinctive taste; some people disliked it, I was one that quite liked it – it was just different to a real egg. It was at the time mostly used for cakes or batters, etc.

Chapter Fourteen

c.1945-1951: Post-war

The war eventually came to an end, but not food rationing; for a while the rations were actually cut. Coal and anthracite were rationed too. Those were still delivered by horse and cart and at least one of us had to watch and count the sacks being brought in, because there was quite a lot of cheating at the time: the delivery men could keep back one sack if there were a lot on the flat-back cart. They always made a great show of folding the sack as they went out and flopping it onto a pile. But it was easy enough for them to slip a prepared empty onto the pile, so if they were counted by a housewife who thought her delivery looked very small, there were the right empties. Or, before the cart left the depot, a few lumps could be taken from each bag to make an extra one for their own home, or for selling 'on the side'. I don't think we were often cheated, but there were so many different delivery men, and one couldn't get to know them all.

We knew the butcher's delivery man who came with a pony and specially-cooled covered trap, but, a while after the war started, the butcher stopped delivering and, like most other food, we carried it back from the shop. Milk, strictly rationed, was always delivered. The milkman, either disabled or too old for war service, drove and juggled the bottles around, and most of the running down the many passages between houses to the back doors was done by boys who could leave school at fourteen, and later fifteen years old. We had one milkman for years who liked our cats and, after the war, when we went away for a very few days, volunteered to pour a little into the cat's saucer, but our neighbour had already volunteered to feed the pussies – we just had to arrange for a half-pint to be delivered.

The gas meter reader was a tiny man with a hunched shoulder. My mother always had a friendly chat when he came round, as regular as clockwork though I think he 'did' the whole town, shops and all. One week he didn't come (it might have been fortnightly). When he next came, my mother said she hoped she hadn't missed his ring because she was in. He started to say something, broke down and came over a bit wobbly so my mother got him indoors, sat him down and made him tea. He said he had been waiting till he got to our house because he wanted to tell someone, and our mother was so kind and understanding he wanted to tell her first – his wife had died, and he had needed a few days off work! There were a few shops in the town that had basements and he would have to use the lift, not mechanised but made to go up and down by the passenger hauling on a rope with pulleys. A few years later, he was using one of these lifts when he had a heart attack. He returned to work after a while, but soon after that retired or died.

When we moved to Bedford we used to send bed sheets to the laundry as there was really no drying place for large washing indoors in winter. It was collected in a box like a suitcase and brought back and put on the doorstep if one was out. Every so often, a man came round for us to pay the bill. One day, I was home with my mother, Sheila was out for some reason, and the post came so our mother sat down in the dining room where we had been about to start a brass cleaning session. Auntie Lil was the best correspondent of our mother's sisters, but that day there was a letter from Auntie Vera (Joan and Phyllis' mother) and my mother opened it eagerly. Next minute she said, 'My Gert is dead, she has had a brain haemorrhage like our mother and she is dead!'[1] It was Gert who had mothered all the family from the time she was sixteen. My mother burst into sobs and I put my arms around her. At that very moment, the laundry man came in the back gate and along the passage and rang the back door bell. Getting no answer, he looked around and saw us through the French doors/windows. He put his head on one side and pointed to the back door as he came back towards us. I shook my head violently and pointed to the back gate and he nodded and went out quickly and quietly. Later, she remarked how odd, the laundryman hadn't been and I said, 'I expect he will tell you next time he comes, probably missed us by mistake or just got late, or was ill'. When he did come next time, she asked about his missed visit and I have always thought he must have been a sensitive man; he gave a believable reason, but not the truth.

There were no supermarkets when we were

---

1 Gertrude Lena Lang (née Pope) died in Vernon, British Columbia, on 18 January 1940. See *British Columbia, Canada, Death Index, 1872-1990*.

young, just small local shops. The greengrocers was run by a husband and wife; the husband's brother delivered on his cycle. He eventually had to give up the cycling but, by that time, we were old enough to ride our cycles down and collect what our mother ordered, or call in and collect things on our way back from school. Most households made their own jam and marmalade, and there was a special extra ration of sugar at jam-making time. The greengrocer's wife had an orange slicer and she would lend it to some of her customers, the ones she trusted and knew would bring it back after the one or two agreed days.

I remember the chemist's wife too, almost the last shop before the long walk up Goldington Road. She became a good friend after my mother had told her that her own father had been a chemist. All shops had a chair, or chairs, by their counter so customers could sit while they placed their orders and, if other customers came in, the chemist's wife would tell our mother, just keep sitting there and rest before you tackle Goldington Road and on home. As the years went by, she knew our mother had a lot of trouble with her back and was often in considerable pain – and carrying shopping bags doesn't help backs, hips or knees as I found out years later! When our mother died, the greengrocer's wife and the chemist's wife came to her funeral, probably the first time I had seen them outside their shops! Their attendance was much appreciated, and so many other people in the town said kind things about her to us, it does comfort bereaved people somehow.

One other memory of the shops, was the outfitters where all school uniforms were stocked and summer dresses could be made to measure. They also sold fabrics and haberdashery. The first time we went there and ordered something (uniforms for St. Andrew's probably), our mother gave our name and the assistant stopped writing and looked embarrassed. 'I pay when I collect', said our mother, 'I don't want an account'. The assistant looked very relieved, as Granny Kelly was well known in town for having an account and for delaying payment! When Auntie Kathleen came to live with her, she added her purchases to Granny Kelly's account and paying them off took even longer. Uncle Lennie was a good sound-recorder, but unless he was actually making a film, he wasn't being paid; Jennifer went to the convent school in Bedford, Michael went to a school near the south coast (Weybridge possibly). I am thankful that we were brought up to pay as we bought; to be in debt was a terrible thing. You saved till you could afford what you needed or wanted, and you didn't buy anything until you had saved enough.

Sheila had always wanted to be a nurse; ever since she had had scarlet fever she had said that was what she was going to do. At the High School, if one didn't do classics or one of the university subjects, there was a pre-nursing course that could be done along

Figure 112. Sheila when nursing at Tunbridge Wells in 1947

with general subjects in the lower sixth form. (There was also an advanced domestic course and a secretarial course.) Having been plump all her life, she became very thin in her later teens so, though I think she could have left after the fifth-form, it was thought that having a start, a good start, into the theory of nursing, would make the very strenuous first year in hospital less exhausting. (Student nurses did all the ward cleaning in those days.) She wanted to go to Barts,[2] but the matron who interviewed her thought she looked too fragile for the tough regime at Barts, and suggested she tried the hospital in Tunbridge Wells, Kent, where she herself had trained.[3] She was accepted and soon after started her training there. Our mother and I went with her – train to London, taxi to get us across London, and another train to Tunbridge Wells. Apart from my brief visit to Lacock with our father (1936) and Shelia's hospital stays during ear operations, we had hardly ever been apart. Our personalities were different. I had long-before given up discussing or arguing with her if our opinions differed – she always knew better than me because she was one year and three weeks older (which eventually became a joke between us). Her main hobby was knitting and she would sit close to the radio with 'light' music playing all evening, though I (and often our mother) would have preferred silence as we found it easier to concentrate on our books. Sheila also had a little radio on the table between our beds and, as soon as she woke, she put it on; moreover, as soon as she was in bed, she would put it on at night. She usually went to sleep very quickly and then I would turn the radio off and, at last, had a double-quick reading session.

I expect I had equally annoying habits; I know it did frustrate her (and, to a lesser extent, our mother) that I could be so lost in a book or just my thoughts that I didn't hear the first time that either of them spoke to me. Anyway, for whatever reason, the day we all went to Tunbridge Wells, I woke feeling sick but determined to go; I felt worse as we travelled and must have looked it because they kept asking me if I wanted the taxi to stop! After we had seen her to her room and said goodbye, we travelled home and I gradually felt better. The bedroom and sitting room without that background of 'light' music seemed strange, but I suppose we got used to it! In the end, she was only at Tunbridge Wells for four months while she got progressively thinner and more rundown, and she had to give up and return home. It took her another four months to regain her strength and health.

Then, she tried nursing at the north part of Bedford Hospital, which was then in Kimbolton Road. (It had been the old work house and the two main gateposts still had carved onto them, half on each side, 'The poor you have / Always with you'.) A few months

---

2   St. Bartholomew's Hospital in London.
3   Possibly Pembury County Hospital, which opened in 1938 and closed in 2010-2012, when it was replaced by Tunbridge Wells Hospital.

there and she was ill again, so more time at home and then she worked at the Barnardo's Home across the river. Later, she had a job in the food department of the Shire Hall and stayed there until she went to Canada.

I really didn't know what I wanted to do when I left school, so I did the sixth-form secretarial course, plus the main subjects. I would have liked to have gone to university, but the entrance exams all needed Latin, which I had had to give up after our first year at the High School. Having missed the first year that the rest of my class had done, I found it impossible to catch up, though I did try, but presumably wasn't clever enough. I really did try, slogging through the first-year book during one of the holidays I think, because I remember taking it to Auntie Mary's when we visited her for a few days.

While on the secretarial course, I found the typing lessons easy and fun, the shorthand fascinating and I was easily the best at writing accurately: it was the speed that I found difficult. The bookkeeping and accounting was horrible – my columns never seemed to add up and 'double entry' bookkeeping just seemed totally pointless. The commercial geography was the easiest. I had always loved history and geography. Not wishing to boast, but when, in the exam room, we opened our O-levels, we were all taken aback by the questions in the second half of the paper as they had nothing to do with the syllabus. The geography mistress was also taken aback. It was her first year of teaching and she was very upset when she realised she had somehow spent a year teaching us all the wrong syllabus! Confronted with a lot of questions about Australia and sheep farming and general agriculture and their imports and exports, I desperately recalled everything I could that I had ever read or heard about Australia. I suppose some of the other girls 'passed' but I was the only one to get a 'credit'.

When I left school, the war was over or I would have joined the women's army (and probably been a disaster), as we were very short of money. Our father kept cutting down the amount he paid into the bank every month, and writing to us that it was high time we stopped fiddling about in the shelter of home, and the best education was to get out, meet different sorts of people and earn our keep and not be a burden to our mother or him. (Those were some of the milder things he used to write, alas. It was all very hurtful, but we loved him and still hoped he would come back.) So I got a job at the local optician's typing letters, adding up the incomings, wrapping the spectacles when they were posted to patients and other oddments, like shovelling the pavement clear of snow when necessary. My boss was the daughter of an optician and one of the first women to qualify in her own right. £3 a week was pretty pathetic pay even in those days, but it helped at home.

In my last school holidays, I had gone apple-picking up Putnoe Lane for Mr. and

Chapter Fourteen ~ c.1945-1951: Post-war 129

Figure 113. Site of the Bedford Training College, 1882-1969

Mrs. Harrington, and I went every summer when, later, I was at the teacher training college. The Harringtons had a son who was a doctor and had a lot to do with the measles vaccination, which was quite new then. He had been the doctor who actually gave the injection to Prince Charles when he was small. Their daughter had been a ferry pilot during the war and died when her unarmed plane was shot down. The Harringtons employed one boy in the holidays to drive what looked like a rotovator, which pulled a trailer loaded with the boxes of apples we had picked, down to the grading table. There were stools for the graders to perch on and, if any of the girls were feeling a bit under the weather, they were allowed to be a grader all day instead of taking turns. Mrs. Harrington loved 'her' girls and we all had a mug of tea at 'elevenses' time and ate our lunch sandwiches in their kitchen. If anyone was stung by any insect, she would be up to the orchard with the appropriate ointment, or take the girl down to the kitchen for more treatment or just a sit-down. One of the perks of working in the orchard was that we were allowed to take home any of the damaged apples after they had been put on the pile of rejects. Plums and greengages too. At the end of the afternoon, I would load my bike basket and carrier with as much as I could cram in and our mother spent the next day jam and jelly making. The sugar was an expense of course, but the end product was more nourishing – and cheaper than shop-bought. I really enjoyed the fruit-picking weeks and, in my last year, I was in charge of the girls – not onerous and a little extra pay.

After two and a bit years at the optician's, I decided I would go to the Bedford Training College, which at that time was a three-year course and considered much better than the two-year course at the subsidised government colleges.[4] (See Figure 113.) Also, I could live at home and cycle over to the college every day. In my remaining time at the optician's, I saved as much as I could. My mother and Sheila had generously said I need not contribute to the housekeeping while I was at college and when I started I had in my savings enough for two years' fees. So all I needed to do was earn, somehow, enough for the third year's fees and for my running expenses – they proved to be quite a lot…! So, once a week I cycled home via the vicarage where I typed letters for the vicar. That barely covered the running expenses, so in the summer I went fruit-picking for every day possible (and prayed we would not be rained off), and, in the Easter holidays, I helped issue the new ration books for which the food department took on extra staff. That was dull, but occasionally I would be part of a team that went round the villages (by taxi) if they were too remote for the villagers to get to the Shire Hall.

In the Christmas holidays, I was a temporary post-delivery worker, and that was fun too. I remember delivering the length of Bushmead Avenue. I discovered that a lot of the iron stairs to the top floors of the large houses were not fire escapes as I had always thought, but the entrances to flats. One side of the avenue had more than the other so we left the staircase side till we had lightened the load a bit. The bags started off quite heavy and we were not allowed to put them down anywhere, so we had to heave them up and down flights of stairs – they were lighter than boxes of apples anyway! There was no ration-book work in my last Easter holiday as rationing had, by then, been abolished.[5] This was a bit of a financial disaster for me, but I had saved just enough for the third year except for the running expenses, so the typing for the vicar was even more necessary. Our dear old Mr. Down had gone to Belize some years before,

---

[4] The Bedford Training College had been established as the Kindergarten School in January 1882. It was originally located at 34 Bromham Road, but soon relocated to 14 The Crescent. The college began with five students and expanded quickly, remaining at the same location for over seventy years. For more information on the school see: http://www.beds.ac.uk/howtoapply/departments/teacher-education/history

[5] Rationing lasted in Britain until 4 July 1954.

Chapter Fourteen ~ c.1945-1951: Post-war

Figures 114 and 115. Shelia and Daphne on their trip to visit Canadian relations in 1953, Daphne is wearing the coat given to her by Sheila, in both its belted and flared mode (which came in so useful later!) (CMFR)

Figure 116. RMS Empress of Japan (later Scotland), c.1930

Daphne and Shelia returned from their trip to Canada, arriving in Liverpool on 4 September 1953 aboard the (second) RMS Empress of Scotland, having sailed from Montreal, Canada. The RMS Empress of Japan (as the ship was originally christened) was built at Goven on the Clyde in 1929-1930 by Fairfield Shipbuilding for the Canadian Pacific Steamships; in 1942, it was renamed the RMS Empress of Scotland, the second ship of that name. It came in at 25,000 gross tons and could carry 1173 passengers.

and his successor was the Revd. Mr. Fox. Mr. Fox eventually moved on and was followed by the Revd. John Hare (1912-1976), who later married us and later still served as Archdeacon of Bedford (1962-1973) and Suffragan Bishop of Bedford (1969-1976).

The Froebel training taught at the college was then considered in the forefront of teaching methods,[6] but the staff had some strange ideas, to my mind. Except for the sewing and handicraft teacher who was lovely and sensible (I am glad I did the advanced sewing course), the staff were forever telling us we must 'liberate children' from their desks, from discipline, apparently from sitting down or bothering to listen to a teacher till they felt they wanted to! Most of the staff seemed to be anti-Christian which was difficult sometimes, but I didn't go on Sunday outings or whatever it was until I had been to church, and that was that. Their ideas about 'liberating' children had disastrous consequences for some of the students when we went out on teaching practices, and some girls finished up in tears and collapsed and had to be started in another school. I would arrange my classrooms in a fairly 'liberated' way – no table or desks facing the teacher – and have plenty of activities going on during the staff visits, but exerted gentle discipline at other times as, after some of the students' visits, the staff had a really hard time getting the children to work properly – and happily – again. I was fortunate that one of the staff who supervised me in my final teaching practice was the one under whom I had enjoyed the sewing and handicrafts.

I didn't have any new clothes while I was at college. I had two winter skirts when I started, the one had been made by Aunt Elsie when I was fifteen I think, and the other was a hand-me-down. So, too, was my winter coat, a sort of hairy blue thing. Trousers were not allowed for women, even when cycling to village schools which could be seven or more miles away. The skirts were worn somewhat paper-thin by the end of three years and the coat wore right through the cuffs during my second year and most of the 'hairy' had worn off the back where it rubbed on my cycle saddle.

At some stage, when Sheila and I were down in the town, we looked in the clothes shop window and chatted about which coat we liked most and, to my total surprise, the one I had thought the nicest appeared at Christmas as a very generous present from Sheila. (See Figures 114 and 115.) I wore it for years and took it to Germany with us after we were married. I did then have a fitted and possibly more fashionable overcoat, but that was the trouble – it fitted. The dear old coat was flared and had a belt through slots in the side seams, and adapted nicely to the bump that became Charles, and the bump that became Wendy. I think it was my coming-back-to-England coat

---

[6] That method of education devised by the German reformer, Friedrich Froebel (1782-1852), which emphasized the development of the whole child. He is best remembered for his establishment of kindergarten.

after Malaya and eventually, worn-out only in parts (I had worn it as a winter dressing gown as well!), I cut it up and made a dressing gown for Charles – and, in time, everyone else! Sheila also generously knitted me a jumper for other occasions, and that must have been expensive too as 'batwing' sleeves were then fashionable.

Chapter Fifteen

c.1950-1951:
Death of Father, Teaching and Marriage

It was in July 1950, during my third year at college, that our father died.[1] In his letters, he had been describing the hardships of living in Jerusalem.[2] They had there a fairly primitive flat with outside stairs and some sort of flat roof, where they sat if it was not too cold or dusty or hot. He kept saying how they liked living there, free from the restrictive life of England and all the 'bigotry', etc., etc. Also how he admired the Jews for their hard work and love of freedom – and the Arabs quite the opposite – and the dangerous state that everything was in was Britain's fault, etc. They had endured the 'siege' of Jerusalem when all foreigners were evacuated except for two or three, but he was there unofficially and didn't want to leave.

There was no post from him for six months and we wrote to the Red Cross to try to get news, but they didn't find anything about him. Eventually, he wrote and chided us for being worried; he knew he would be safe as he/they had so many Jewish friends, ones who loved them so much they even invited him to their Passover-festival meal, which was a compliment and a sign that they would count you as their own if there was trouble. It was a terrible time there as Palestine tried to turn

---

1 Edward Kelly actually died during Daphne's second (not third) year in college. Very probably the confusion lies in the unimaginable delay that occurred before the family received notification of his death (see details below).

2 Edward Kelly, who lived at the fashionable address of 231 Street of the Prophets in Jerusalem, died of pneumonia on 6 July 1950 at the French Hospital in Jerusalem, and was buried with military honors in the American Cemetery of the German colony near Jerusalem. Probate, handled by his solicitors in Leicester, disclose that he left an estate of £2503 10s. 8d. No record of his heir has been uncovered. See Index of Wills and Administrations for England and Wales, 1951. A brief biographical account of Edward's life and career written by his brother, Arthur, has been included in Appendix II

itself into Israel, a country for Jews and their chosen few, which did not include Arabs.

After the six months' siege we had letters from him, but not many.[3] He was too tired coping with their food shortages and apparently carrying all the water they needed in buckets up the outside stairs to the flat. (What was the woman doing all this time? Apparently nothing to help him.) There was inflation everywhere and he took a clerical job in the financial department of the Israeli police. He was so tired he kept having little dozes at his desk. One day, the others couldn't wake him: he had gone into a diabetic coma. He was taken to hospital, sorted out, and sent home, but it was too soon: back in the flat he developed pneumonia, was taken back to hospital, but his temperature kept going up and his heart couldn't stand the strain and he died. He had written to us not long before stating that he was so tired of the bitter winters, the too-hot summers and everything else – that even England seemed preferable at times. Of course, we latched onto those ideas and a glimmer of hope returned to us – you might wonder how, if you read the few letters I have kept (written in his mauve ink, because the world was so dreary why make it worse with black ink!)

One day, Sheila was dressing carefully as she was going to visit Aunt Elsie (then a 'Dame' at Eton) as her guest at the College's Fourth of June celebrations.[4] Our mother must have heard the post come and, as I came out of the bathroom at the top of the stairs, I saw her coming up, holding the banisters with her left hand and flapping a letter in her right, not immediately looking at me but whispering, 'It says he is dead, my Edward is dead'. (This was in 1951, my third year of college.)[5] It was the first time she had ever used his Christian name speaking to either of us, and she looked so ill that I pulled her into the bathroom, sat her on the edge of the bath and held her close. 'Look, read it; it says he is dead, doesn't it?' All the letter said was, 'Owing to the death of your husband, all payments from his account are stopped until his affairs are cleared up'. We sat on the edge of the bath and wondered if it was really true. Then we thought of Sheila, preparing for a rare day off and away; if we told her, she wouldn't feel like going to Eton, but there wasn't anything she could do immediately. I was going to walk to the station with Sheila and see her off, pushing my bike so I could cycle home. 'Can you get to the station with her without her noticing that anything is wrong?' whispered our mother. 'Yes', I replied. So we hurried her through breakfast, with our mother mostly hiding in the kitchen, and I walked with her as fast as I could and cycled

---

3 This probably refers to the Battle for Jerusalem, which took place between December 1947 and mid-July 1948.

4 Which celebrates the birthday of King George III, Eton's greatest patron.

5 This occurred virtually a year after the death of Edward Kelly on 6 July 1950 – an astonishing amount of time to have passed before this vital information reached Daphne's mother. Remarkably, no one in Jerusalem (including the Jewish authorities or Mrs. Bastyan) saw fit to inform Edward's widow and children of his death.

back home.

I phoned the college and said why I wouldn't be in for two or three days, and we phoned our mother's solicitor in London. I think it was the next day we went together to see him, and he put the wheels in motion and, eventually, we heard officially that Edward Kelly was definitely dead. The two fares to London took about all the cash in the house, till Sheila's next payday or until I typed for the vicar! We sold various bits of brass and things they had brought back from China (there was a second-hand shop next to the greengrocer), and I think it was about three months before any money came in again. We wrote to the executors in Israel and asked for his personal things, including all the photograph albums we had sent out at his request years before, when he said he felt lonely and would like their company. He had also asked for his record collections to be shipped out and various other things. After a long time, we were told that there were so many debts to be settled before 'the woman' could leave the country, that every single thing had been sold. I know she did come back to live somewhere in Britain and spent her time getting drunk. She wrote one letter to our mother saying how sad she was and how she didn't know what she was going to do without him. Our mother looked through it once then gently and deliberately tore it up and burnt it, saying only, 'How dare she…'

Eventually, her widow's pension came through: it was tiny, but at least it was regular. Later on, a helpful sum came, apparently from a benevolent fund associated with the Regiment. When I told Michael about that many years later, he looked quite shocked and said that was only for 'other ranks' and non-commissioned officers. Maybe it was a tactful way for some of his old friends to help her; it certainly contained condolences from friends in general – 'knowing how difficult things could be in the first few months'. Our Auntie Kathleen Birkett, widow of dear Uncle Norman who had died of cancer a few years before, sent, trustingly, in her first letter after the family had been told, a £5 note which was a generous chunk of her widowhood income. News somehow got around.

One day the landlord, who lived in Great Barford and almost never appeared despite our occasional requests that he pay for painting the outside of the house (Sheila and I even cycled to Great Barford a couple of times), appeared on the doorstep and said how sorry he was to hear of the death and, if we found it difficult to pay the rent, he would be happy to wait a few weeks for it as we had always done it 'on the dot'. Fortunately the rent was still 'fixed' and we managed without owing anything to him or anyone. As soon as I was earning, Sheila and I went to the pensions department at the Shire Hall and made enquiries about the voluntary scheme into which my mother had, in theory, been paying. One had to pay for four years before receiving a small pension.

*Figure 117. Grave of Edward Rupert Kelly,
American (now International) Cemetery of the German Colony, near Jerusalem*

She was rather in arrears and we filled the gap, and then, I think, bought the weekly stamps between us. She only had a few weeks to go when she died.

We had our father's name and details put on the Kelly grave in Bedford graveyard. Later, we buried our mother's ashes there on the side where his name was and had hers put on as well. I have never seen his grave in Israel. When he died, Jerusalem was still partitioned and he couldn't be buried in the British cemetery, so his friends took him to the American cemetery. They knew he had been in the British army, but no one knew what Christians did at the funerals of their loved ones, but they found a Union Flag from somewhere and draped it over the coffin, took their police rifles and fired a '*feu du mort*' as they lowered the coffin, and that was all. Many years later, our cousin Apphia (with her husband Michael) found herself near the cemetery while they were on holiday (it had been expanded to be the international cemetery by then), and she took the two pictures I have. I would like to see his grave, but probably won't. It will all be sorted out one day in heaven.

Not very many years ago, long after I had thought I had given up having dreams about him, I had one more dream. I had been looking for him for a long time and finally tracked him down to where he was sitting in a wheelchair and looking incredibly old – as he would have been – and he whispered, 'I've been waiting such a long time, I knew you would come. I wanted you so much, I am sorry, do you forgive me?' I put my arms round him and he relaxed and died. It was strange. We had some letters from a few of his Jewish friends saying how much they had loved him. They knew he had a wife and children somewhere, but he had never confided to anyone what a mess his life was. He was very obstinate, much too prone to flattery and, I suppose, he was very selfish. He was also fascinating and talented, and we loved him very much.

Our mother was loved by everyone who knew her. So many would come to her for comfort or counsel knowing that a secret told to her would remain a secret, and personal problems would stay between the two of them; all sorts of problems – I can't say what they were because they remained with her only.

Our mother's back gave her permanent trouble and eventually her heart began to wear out. Sheila continued to work at the Food Office. I taught and, after four years of teaching, married – and family history after that can be seen on the videos and DVD Daddy will finish one day!

Figure 118. A happier picture to finish, which I took in May 1956, when we were engaged. Shelia, Daphne, and Muriel Kelly (CMFR)

Postlude: The Beginning of the Future

Figure 119. Daphne Muriel Kelly in 1955 (then aged 27) at the wedding of her cousin, James; this is where I first met her. James and I were commissioned into the Essex Regiment at the same time, in 1952; by 1955, we were both serving at the Regimental Depot at Warley, Essex. She and Sheila nearly didn't come to the wedding, as Sheila had singed her eyebrows off that morning when the gas oven exploded! After the wedding they had dashed off early to catch the train home before I even knew her name: I had to wait three weeks for James to return from his honeymoon before I could ask who she might be. I knew she was a cousin, which narrowed it down to three! He thought it could be Daphne - but wasn't sure. Anyway, I wrote to her inviting her to a Regimental Ball – and the right girl arrived at St Pancras station. It was a nervous wait! Another close call for your existence! (CMFR)

Appendix I

A Brief History of Peachland, British Columbia
(from: *Peachland Memories, 1820-1939*, Peachland Museum, Peachland, B.C.)

The Okanagan native culture reached its peak 3000 years ago. At that time archeologists estimate that about 12,000 people lived in the valley and surrounding areas, including the Arrow Lakes, Washington State and Merritt/Nicola area. The language spoken was Interior Salish. One of the unique distinguishing characteristics of this period is the winter house or 'Pit house'. It has many similar sounding names but the most common is kekuli. They were built by digging a one-metre deep, square or round hole in the ground and erecting 4 poles for roof support. The roof was covered in wood, bark, and then covered in sod. The entrance was down a carved log stairway through the centre roof hole. They would be warm in winter with animal skins and woven mats on the floor. Of course, the central fire smoke exited through the hole in the roof. Most of these pit house (winter) sites have been destroyed by recent development. Old timers remember a site near the present Peachland shopping center where there were 3 large holes left from kekulis. Archeologists have recorded 200 such sites in the Kamloops area. You may see a reconstruction of one at the Kelowna Museum. When the weather warmed, a more portable type of shelter was used consisting of an A frame or similar shape with a woven mat cover laid on framework to shed rain and provide shade.

The first non-natives to discover the site were fur traders who ventured north from Fort Okanagan on the Columbia River in the early 1800's. These fur traders came with pack horses and travelled as far north as Fort

Kamloops on the Thompson River. Loaded pack trains returned to Fort Okanogan and the furs were loaded on sailing ships which sailed to Europe.

Gold was discovered in California in the 1840's and this caused a stampede of prospectors to search for the precious mineral throughout the mountains of western North America. These prospectors searched the Okanagan Mountains and creeks and enjoyed the beautiful warm valley landscape surrounding Okanagan Lake.

About 1880, a few hardy settlers found arable land near the shores of Okanagan Lake and started to raise cattle and plant crops. The Canadian Pacific Railway completed its commitment to build a railway from the Atlantic Ocean to the Pacific Ocean across Canada in 1885. Okanagan settlers welcomed this railway because they could drive their mature cattle to Kamloops for loading onto trains to go to markets in eastern Canada. The CPR was pleased with the extra business and realised that the Okanagan was a potential increased revenue source. A branch line was extended south from Sicamous to Vernon on the Okanagan Lake and a steamship SS Aberdeen launched to supply residents along the shores of the Lake with regular service.

The Fur Brigade Trail passed through Peachland on a very long route from the mouth of the Columbia River in Oregon to the fur trading area of northern British Columbia. The furs were gathered from the native people in the summer and carried back by the same route to be shipped from Astoria, Oregon, to England by sailing ship. In 1811, the first fur traders passed through and established a trading post at today's Kamloops, where two rivers meet. Both the Pacific Fur Company and the North West Company traded until 1821, and then amalgamated with the famous Hudson's Bay Company. From 1826 until 1847 when the Oregon U.S. boundary settlement established the American boundary, the trail was very well used by hundreds of horses laden with trade goods. Scouts would go ahead to prepare a site for the night's camp.

The trail was well established and used after 1860 by the prospectors searching for gold. In this area the trail came down to Deep Creek from Summerland's Garnet Lake, crossing Deep Creek and staying above the lake (Renfrew Road) level, away from the heavy lakeshore brush and trees. A noted stop was at May Springs just below the intersection of Princeton and Somerset Avenue, beside the old Pierce home, later the Des and Peggy Loan property, at the end of Princess Street. The trail crossed Trepanier Creek close to the mountain and angled up the mountain to pass beside Hardy's Lake and down the other side to the great flat at Westbank. There is now a large cairn at Old Okanagan Highway and Highway 97 dedicated to the Historic Fur Brigade Trail.

Long ago another important trail went west up the present Princeton Avenue. For hundreds of years the native people used this 'Indian Trail' in summer to travel and trade with other natives from the interior and coast. They were also getting a supply of red ochre at today's Princeton (Vermillion Forks). The red earth was used for pictographs, decoration and even face paint. This trail was later used to supply the huge gold rush town of Granite Creek, near Princeton. As a result it became known as the Granite City Road. Equipment and supplies coming to the north end of the lake by CPR rail were moved by boat and packhorses up this road to the gold rush. Granite City was then the fourth largest town, by population, in British Columbia. In 1893, J.M. Robinson improved this road part way as a wagon road to open the Kathleen Mine in the hills above his gold rush town of Glen Robinson. Alas, the gold did not pan out and it became the 'gold rush town that never was'.

A single picture taken there in 1899 exists showing a group of young people, including teacher Charlie Elliot. His name appears many times in the early history of Peachland.

Today the ghost town site is about a mile north of Glen Lake. The deep canyon route that descends to Okanagan Lake was then called 'The Glen Road' – today it is Princeton Avenue, and was first traversed by car in May of 1931. The car was pulled over a logging road by horses a short way, then it traveled a dirt road from Osprey Lake to Princeton.

The first record of mining in Peachland is by the Camp Hewitt Mining and Development Company, which in 1887 was following a promising lead near the south side of the Pincushion Mountain. When John Moore Robinson and Harry Hardy came to the area in 1888, Robinson was aware of all the gold mining activity in British Columbia and this developing mine looked like a good prospect. He formed the Canadian - American Gold Mining Co. and purchased the claim from Gus Hewitt, the owner. The camp for the Gladstone mine was at the bottom of the Camp Hewitt spring (south end of Ponderosa Golf Course).

John Moore Robinson stopped at a log cabin beside Trepanier Creek, the first residence built in Peachland, and enjoyed some ripe peaches from a tree planted in the yard. John saw a future for fruit growing in the Okanagan Valley, and returned to his Manitoba home where he convinced some of his investor friends to put up funds to purchase land and sub-divide orchard lots. He named the area Peachland and soon settlers arrived and planted orchards. The community grew and sawmills were built to make lumber to build the homes for the newly arrived settlers. The Post Office opened for business on December 1st 1898, and a one room school opened the same year.

The community prospered and a larger four room school was built in 1908, an octagonal Baptist Church in 1910, a Methodist Church in 1911, and a Presbyterian Church in 1912. In the same year the new school was built, the Anglican Church opened in the old one room school house. During this time, many orchards were planted and flourished.

A cannery and packing houses were constructed on the shore and commerce increased, with larger vessels, SS Okanagan and SS Sicamous, providing daily weekday service to Okanagan residents from Penticton to Vernon. On January 1st 1909, the young community became incorporated as the Corporation of the District of Peachland and was able to issue debentures to raise money to construct a dam and electricity generating facility on Trepanier Creek.

The community had grown to 200 and a Regatta was held each year, starting in 1908, with Peachland's War Canoe teams successfully defending its wins each year up until the Great War began in 1914. This tiny community answered the Call to Arms and sent thirty-three young men off to war in Europe. When the war ended in 1918 only eighteen returned, and Peachland had the sad honour of having the greatest per-capita loss of any Canadian town. To remember those who gave the greatest sacrifice, a cenotaph was erected in 1921, and still is a respected reminder of human conflict. Additional names have been added to honour those who died in the Second World War and the Korean War.

After the Great War was over, veterans returned to Peachland and worked in the orchards and sawmills as the community continued to grow. The great depression of the 1930s was severe, however, as orchards failed and prosperity seemed so far away. Work was scarce and most residents were forced to do some belt-tightening to survive. Slowly, the economy recovered and Canada was cheered with a Royal Visit in 1939. However, storm clouds were gathering over Europe, and before the year was out Canada was once again at War with Germany.

Appendix II

Biographical Account of Edward Rupert Kelly

by Arthur Hamilton Kelly [1]

Edward Rupert Kelly was the second son of Lieutenant Colonel Thomas James Pearce Kelly, and was born on 13th September 1891, being educated at Bedford School and Keble College, Oxford.

He was to take Holy Orders, but with the coming of the Great War, he entered the Army, and on 1st February 1915, he was gazetted Temporary 2nd Lieutenant, being posted to the 9th Battalion of the Welch Regiment. He underwent training at Weston-super-Mare, and Perham Down, and was sent to the 12th Reserve Battalion at Kinmel Park, North Wales, in July 1915.

He re-joined the 9th Welch in France in September 1915, and became the Battalion Bombing Officer, being dangerously wounded in the Brigade bombing attack at La Boisselle, on the 2nd July 1916. A bullet entered his right cheek, fracturing the jaw, and tearing the muscles round the right shoulder blade. From hospital at Rouen, to St. Agnes' hospital in Grosvenor Square, he went finally to the Convalescent Hospital at Luton Hoo, and remained on sick leave until June 1917, when he re-joined the 3rd Reserve Battalion at Redcar, Yorkshire.

On 1st July 1917, he was promoted Temporary Lieutenant, and obtained a Regular Commission in the Essex Regiment, dating from the 4th August 1916.

He re-joined the 9th Welch in France in November 1917, and was in the Cambrai area when he was wounded again. This time it was

---

[1] Arthur Hamilton Kelly (1903-1961) was the brother of Edward Rupert Kelly, and the father of Apphia and James Kelly.

in the arm, but he was only away from the Battalion for two weeks, and was back in the line at the time of the great German onslaught in 1918.

In the retreat that followed, he was wounded yet a third time, outside Bapaume on 26th March 1918, on this occasion in the leg, and with difficulty reached the last hospital train in that unfortunate area.

He returned to the 3rd Welch in June 1918, at Redcar, and in September transferred to the 3rd Essex at Felixstowe.

In October of the same year, he was appointed Adjutant to the 15th Battalion of the Regiment in France, and was with them in the final advance up to the day of the Armistice. He was promoted Temporary Captain on 16th February 1919, but in June of that year he joined the 2nd Battalion at Colchester as Lieutenant and was later posted to the Regimental Depot at Warley, where he remained until the completion of his tour of duty on 4th November 1921.

On leaving the Depot he joined the 1st Battalion in Ireland, being stationed at the time of the Irish Armistice at Bandon, near Cork, and later at Fort Charles, Kinsale. During the trouble in the North, he was with the Battalion at Carrickfergus, Belfast, and came over with it to Quebec Barracks, Bordon, in September 1922.

It was in the following month, when on leave, that he met with a motor accident which resulted in the amputation of his right leg above the knee. Six months later he joined the Royal Army Pay Corps on probation, and the appointment was in due course confirmed. He served at Warley, Hounslow, Eastern Command (Horse Guards) and Winchester, being promoted to the rank of Captain.

In July 1924, he married Muriel Vida Birkett at Chislehurst, and, in April 1927, his elder daughter, Sheila Kathleen, was born. His second daughter, Daphne Muriel, was born in May of the following year.

He sailed for Shanghai with the China Defence Force, landing in October 1928, and spent five months in the Command Office there. In March 1929, he was sent to Tientsin, his family joining him, and he returned home in December 1931.

He was next posted to Leamington, and, a few years later, was sent up to the Northern Command at York.

He was promoted successively to the rank of Major and Lt. Colonel, and, early in 1939, was posted abroad again, this time to Palestine, being stationed at the Pay Office in Jerusalem.

Early in 1940, some months after the outbreak of the Second World War, he returned home and spent some time at Southampton, being there during the heavy air raids. Next he was posted to London, when the raids on the capital were at their height, and he remained there until July 1943.

His next move was to the Pay Office at Leicester, which was his final station before his retirement from the Army in 1946. His promotion to Lieutenant-Colonel Staff Paymaster occurred in October 1940.

He received the War Medal 1914-1918, the Victory Medal 1914-1918, the General Service Middle East Medal with Clasp for 'Palestine', the 1939-1945 Campaign Star, the Defence Medal, and the War Medal 1939-1945.

On his retirement in 1946, after thirty-one years in the service, he returned to Palestine, and settled in Jerusalem, in a house near the Old City and Arab Quarter. His home was practically on the front line during the Arab-Israeli war, and was badly damaged, but he did good work in helping to carry up water and supplies to the Jewish troops at the front.

He later served the Jewish State by working in the finance department of the Israeli Police, but the appalling conditions of starvation in Jerusalem had undermined his health, and, after a short illness, he died of pneumonia on 6th July 1950. He was buried with military honours in the American Cemetery of the German Colony near Jerusalem.

Appendix III

Miscellaneous Correspondence, Articles and Images Relating to the Life of Daphne Randall

Death of Mr. George Pope of Kingston Deverill, Wiltshire, November 1860 (*Salisbury and Winchester Journal*, 10 November 1860)

Melancholy death from drowning. – Mr. George Pope, of Kingston Deverill, came by his death in a very sudden and melancholy manner on Monday last. The lamented gentleman, it appears, left his house on horseback about mid-day, as was his custom, and after spending about an hour and a half in riding around his farm and in giving directions to his labourers, he dismounted, tied his horse up in the vicinity of some new buildings, and proceeded on foot across some fields in the direction of others of his labourers. There is a dead well in one of the fields through which he had to pass; this was but partially covered in, and it is supposed by many that he must have either walked across the well unwittingly, and have been precipitated into it through the giving way of some portion of the imperfect covering, or that in examining the well for some purpose he accidentally slipped into it and was drowned. The family of the deceased, on finding that the time at which he usually returned home had long since elapsed, became somewhat uneasy, and sent to neighbouring houses to inquire for him. No one had seen him but a shepherd boy, who said at three o'clock in the afternoon he saw him walking across the fields. Further search was made, and after a time it was found that the insecure covering of this old well had been much displaced, and on looking down a hat was seen swimming on the top of the water. Grappling hooks were immediately procured, and in a few minutes the worst fears of all were realized. The deceased was found to be quite cold; indeed, he must have been in the water for several hours. The well is about 40 feet deep, and contains 30 feet of water. An inquest was held by George Sylvester, Esq., coroner, on the following Wednesday morning, when a verdict of "Found drowned," was returned. The deceased gentleman was universally respected as a kind master and a good and hearty neighbour, and his loss is most severely felt.

Note: George Pope was Daphne's maternal great-grandfather.

* * *

Memorial to Arthur H. Lang, 1905-1990

by R. W. Boyle

Figure 120.

Geological Survey of Canada (retired), Ottawa, Ontario, Canada

With the death of A. H. Lang in Ottawa on July 19, 1990, in his 86th year, Canada and the world lost an eminent economic geologist, an international expert on Canadian uranium deposits, and a friend to prospectors.

Arthur Hamilton Lang was born July 3, 1905, in Peachland, British Columbia, attended public schools there, and later graduated from the University of British Columbia with a B.A. and M.A. in geology. From UBC, Lang went to Princeton University, where he received his Ph.D. in 1930. His thesis, "Geology and Ore Deposits of Owen Lake Mining Camp, B.C.," was published in the Geological Survey of Canada Summary Report for 1929.

Following graduation from Princeton, Lang joined the Geological Survey of Canada in 1930 as assistant geologist and was assigned field work in the Abitibi gold belt of Quebec, including Chibougamau, Waswanipi Lake, Palmorolle and Taschereau map area. From this work Lang produced several field reports and maps during the period 1932-1936. It was during this time that Lang used bush aircraft for transport and reconnaissance and air photos for the preparation of topographic and geologic maps, all firsts for the Geological Survey of Canada. He also emphasized the use of air photos in prospecting to recognize faults, shear zones, lineaments, and so on, a technique that was soon employed by progressive prospectors throughout Canada.

Soon after the outbreak of World War II, Lang enlisted in the Royal Canadian Air Force, but was demobilized at the request of the Metals Controller who, in 1940 considered his talents more valuable in the search for strategic minerals then being organized by the Geological Survey. Lang was then assigned to field work in British Columbia and Alberta, the results of which were several Geological Survey field reports, some on metal mining areas and others, mainly in Alberta, on potential petroleum and natural gas districts.

Following the war, the government of Canada decided to permit and encourage private prospecting and mining of uranium and other atomic materials. The Geological Survey was chosen by the Atomic Energy Control Board as their agent for correlating the data for prospecting, exploration, testing, and evaluation of uranium prospects and maintaining an inventory of all Canadian uranium and thorium deposits. All this work was organized under the Radioactive Resources Division of the Survey with H. V. Ellsworth as chief and Arthur Lang as geologist in charge of field operations and inventory. After Ellsworth's death in 1952, Lang became chief of the division. Later, this division became the Mineral Deposits Division of which he remained chief until his retirement in 1970. During his tenure as chief of the Mineral Deposits Division, Lang wrote several papers on radioactive materials and published a metallogenic map of uranium in Canada, a project, as far as I know, that was a first in metallogenesis. Thereafter he encouraged others in the division to prepare similar metallogenic maps of the other metals.

Following his retirement from the Geological Survey, Arthur Lang undertook part-time contracts with Parks Canada for the preparation of geological guidebooks for several national parks. Four of these guidebooks have been published.

Lang published more than 100 reports, maps, and books on various aspects of Canadian geology and economic geology. He served as secretary of the symposium committee for the first volume of *Structural Geology of Canadian Ore Deposits*, published in 1948, wrote two papers for the volume, and acted as editor for others. In all of his writing he was precise, concise, clear, and factual; he emphasized field geology in economic geology and had little time for theory. His most important economic geology publication was "Canadian Deposits of Uranium and Thorium" (1962), written with J. W. Griffith and H. R. Steacy. This was the first comprehensive compilation of uranium and thorium deposits in Canada—indeed, in any country in the world.

His other famous publication was *Prospecting in Canada* (1970). This publication has sold more copies than any other report of the Geological Survey; it has been used extensively by prospectors, and parts have been utilized in adult education and high school studies. It has been translated by several countries and used as a textbook in the International Atomic Energy Agency in Vienna.

Arthur Lang was particularly cognizant of the role of the Geological Survey in the economy of Canada, and he wrote and lectured on this subject. In one cost/benefit analysis he was able to show as of 1968 that 1.8% of the value of the Elliott Lake uranium deposits, the discovery and development of which the GSC had aided in many ways, would pay the entire operating cost of the GSC since its inception in 1842.

Lang was a bachelor and a very private person, especially in his later years. He was most fastidious in his habits, as I was to learn when, as his assistant in the Northwest Territories, I was lectured on how to maintain a "sparkling" frying pan in a bush camp. He was always interested in the natural environment when he was in the field; he knew much about plants and the various types of mosses and lichens, and he was an expert on Canadian birds. He skied from age 10 to age 80 and was an avid golfer after his retirement.

Arthur Lang was elected a Fellow of the Geological Society of America in 1947 and a Fellow of the Royal Society of Canada in 1951. He was a member of the 50 Year Club of the Canadian Institute of Mining and Metallurgy. He has been honored by the Geological Survey of Canada by the "Lang Lecture" given each year by an eminent economic geologist at their Minerals Colloquium.

Note: Arthur Lang was Daphne's first cousin.

Selected Bibliography of A. H. Lang

1930 Owen Lake Mining Camp, British Columbia: Geological Survey of Canada Summary Report, 62-91.
1933 Palmarolle and Taschereau map areas, Abitibi County, Quebec: Geological Survey of Canada Summary Report, 1932, Part D, 22-35.
1936 Keithley Creek map area, Cariboo District, B. C.: Geological Survey of Canada Paper 36-15.
1940 Houston map area, British Columbia: Geological Survey of Canada Paper 40-18.
1942 Manson Creek, British Columbia: Geological Survey of Canada Paper 42-02.
1946 Brule and Entrance map areas, Alberta: Geological Survey of Canada Memoir 244.
1958 Metallogenic map: Uranium in Canada: Geological Survey of Canada, A Series Map 1045A-M1.
1961 A preliminary study of Canadian metallogenic provinces: Geological Survey of Canada Paper 60-23.

_____. Metallogenic maps: Economic Geology, v. 56, no. 6, p. 1123-1132.

1962 On the relation of metal occurrences to tectonic divisions of the Canadian Shield, in Tectonics of the Canadian Shield: Royal Society of Canada Special Publication 4, 16-21.

_____. (and Griffith, J. W., and Steacy, H. R.) Canadian deposits of uranium and thorium (second edition): Geological Survey of Canada, Economic Geology Series No. 16,324.

1970 Prospecting in Canada (fourth edition): Geological Survey of Canada, Economic Geology Report No. 7,308.

1974 Guide to the geology of Prince Albert National Park; A story of hills, lakes and beaches: Geological Survey of Canada Miscellaneous Report No. 21, 40.

1979 (and Ruzicka, V.) Some geological side-effects of the search for radioactive minerals in the Canadian Shield, in Kupsch, W. O., and Sarjeant, W.A.S., eds., History of concepts *in* Precambrian geology, Geological Association of Canada Special Paper 19, 133-148.

Appendix III ~ Miscellaneous Correspondence

A letter written by Daphne in 1994, prior to her first letter to the surviving members of her family, but to be read, 'Only when I am dead!'

To all my darlings, born, chosen and in-laws and my beloved husband if he is still around!

I couldn't bear the thought of being in heaven without all of you or waiting a long time 'til you came, but I think eternity is not time stretching into infinity, but the present lasting for timelessness, and so even as we see face to face our beloved Lord Jesus and all the loved ones who have gone before us, we shall somehow at the same 'time' find we are joined by – and are one with – all who come after us. In other words we shall not have to suffer any waiting. I hope so anyway!

No one is perfect and we all make mistakes and I've probably made heaps more than I can see, but you are my darlings and I love you all so much. Carry on loving each other and keep in contact however many miles separate you and I shall be loving you wherever I am!

Kisses and hugs to you all,

Mummie xxxxxxxx

* * *

A Letter to all the Family

Written by Daphne Randall on 21st June 2005, to be read, 'only when I'm dead or permanently incapable of expressing myself sensibly'.

In case I ever fall off my twig unexpectedly or become incapable of speaking what is in my mind, I am doing what everyone should do (and it might even grow into an expanded and improved family history which I wrote some years ago)...I love you all, children, spouses and grandchildren so much. Some people learn mostly with their intellects, some through their feelings, some a combination of both, and some learn and remember the look of things and people. Some learn and remember smells, some by the touch of things and people. Christians know Jesus through their intellects, or their feelings, or both. I think a lot more people experience Jesus very directly than talk about it because others may say it is hallucinating, or dreaming or making it up. Some people have that aura about them and you just know they have walked closely with Him for years; for others, it comes and goes (alas), and we are not miraculously and permanently made into better or "nice" people. It is not a dream or a daydream. When we lived in Warminster I had a dream that I was pushing the pram up the High Street and looking at the pavement and saw the feet of someone standing against a wall and I looked up and it was Jesus and I was the only person who recognised Him and I asked Him to come home with us. But He said He had to stay there even if people were unkind to Him. The warmth of that stayed with me for days, together with sadness because I knew it was a dream.

Years later, in Westbury, you were mostly teenagers and I was very depressed and tired and feeling worthless and didn't go to church one Sunday, and didn't feel like it the next Sunday either but thought I had better go. I trailed up to communion and was so slow at putting my hand and head up for communion wine that the vicar, poor chap, passed me by and I thought, "There, I'm so useless and such a nothing that even he can't see me". Time apparently stood still. You know, or perhaps you are not old enough yet to have experienced it, but when you know someone like your husband, or family or friend so well that you can recognise something, or hear a joke or understand something without speaking and then make eye contact and laugh for joy, or contentment or understanding. I heard a laugh, quiet, but love and joy-filled and I looked up from the rail and moving along behind the vicar was Jesus, a man, but I can't say exactly how He looked because He was too Light. He smiled and said, "we don't need the symbols do we?" I wanted to stay there forever, but He was moving along behind the vicar though the others couldn't see Him, so I got up. The peace and joy of it stayed with me for weeks and comes back in blessed moments. As you all know, it hasn't made me a nicer person and I shall probably get more cranky and annoying, but it was not a dream and when the gates of heaven open for me (I hope) I know I shall be in that Presence again.

A P.S. about my idea of heaven – not an eternity of time but totally different; a dimension that will be 'like nothing on earth'. If your spirits are the breath of God we shall be united with Him, through Jesus; united with all our loved ones. We won't be the ages we were when we died, but somehow ageless and somehow 'timeless' before you are all there too; no physical or bodily infirmities, but ageless, recognising spirit, like you can still feel 'one' with your new born babies.

* * *

The Okanagan Valley, by Daphne Randall (28 January 2007):

In case you can 'do' the Okanagan Valley, here are the places that I know Popes lived; but don't expect a beautiful fruit growing region! It was so beautiful that most of the fruit and farming was built over with holiday homes, ski resorts, etc.

When my mother lived there a paddle steamer came once a fortnight with ordered supplies and passengers. By 1953, when we went to Canada on a visit, the paddle steamer Sicamous was beached at the west end of the valley, and being used as a restaurant.

My mother grew up in Peachland, in a home named 'The Vatican' – the house her father, brothers and uncle had built. They went to church in Summerland, and she was married there by the Rector of Peachland, Summerland and roundabout.[1]

Harold lived in Kelowna. Their honeymoon was spent rowing around the lake, exploring parts, and camping at night. A lot of place names are familiar to me, but her sisters lived here and there as they married.

Aunt Vera lived in Nicola. Their father eventually moved into our mother's tiny Vancouver flat after WWI, when she was working as a dental mechanic. When she came to England to marry our father, her father went to live with Aunt Vera, Uncle Frank, Joan and Phyllis in Nicola, but he died six weeks later and our mother felt awful about it for years.

Penticton is very familiar; I think it was where the boat club was located that Harold ran for a while. Don't go there in June, as there is an Elvis Presley lookalike festival (how the mighty have fallen!).

The only fruit I have heard of being grown in the valley now is grapes, which make a wonderful wine after the vines have been frozen solid in winter!

There are roads in all directions now, but then there was only a road on their side of the lake and a dirt track on the other, and no road at all out of the south end.

End of history lesson!

* * *

---

1 Anglican services were held at an early date in Peachland, at the old school house which doubled as a worship space on Sundays. The Rector of Summerland travelled to Peachland to preach, celebrate the Eucharist, and visit the sick and needy. In 1908, when a new (and larger) school was built, a new parish was formed, St. Margaret's, Peachland. The old school house was used as the parish church until 1991, when a new church was built next door; the old school house is now a museum and meeting place. It was at St. Margaret's that Daphne's mother, Muriel, was married to Harold Birkett on 10 April 1912.

Appendix III ~ Miscellaneous Correspondence 161

Figure 121. The Okanagan Valley, looking South from above the town of Naramata

Figure 122. The Okanagan Valley in wintertime

Figure 123. Grapes growing in the Okanagan Valley

Appendix III ~ Miscellaneous Correspondence

Figure 124. The Paddle Steamer Sicamous on the beach at Penticton, Lake Okanagan

Figure 125. Above Peachland (looking south), Lake Okanagan

Figure 126. The Okanagan Valley of British Columbia

A Poem for Auntie Sheila, 2004

When one was 3 and one was 2,
"Oh buckle my shoe, I'm smaller than you."

When 3 was 4 and 2 was 3,
"Run down the garden…" – "Oh wait for me!"

When 4 was 5 and 3 was 4,
"I've caught you, I've caught you! – Let's run some more"

When 5 was 6 and 4 was 5,
They played together, and laughed and cried.

When 6 was 7 and 5 was 6,
School years began, and 6 was alone,

But 'It's easy to read, learn '*and*'
Some sounds you work it out on your own.

S*and* at the seaside, L*and* is the garden
And *band* you can learn when you follow me…

Oh, wait for me!

Different but same, first one then the other
Argue or fight but together unite.
Looked after each other; Dear Father our years
Make the world so hard
75, 76, 77
If you open the gates of heaven for her…
Not long to wait for me.

Note: *This was written in 2004, when Mummie would have been 76 and Auntie Sheila about 77. Its composition may have been prompted by Auntie Sheila not being well, or by Uncle Bryan's death (also c.2004) The original poem has little pictures of two children 'jumping on elm branches, 1931' & 'we climbed up the lilac tree (crossed out, with syringa added) and she cut her leg' + 'He made a sandpit and we planted flowers round' (CMFR)*

*   *   *

Mummie's Poem, 2007 (untitled)

I've shared the garden with the contented snakes,
For 12 years the friendly toad and I kept the
Greenhouse free of slugs and flies;
But oh, I have seen the butterfly shake
Off the drying chrysalis like a soul
About to shed the creaking body and
Fly to glorious heights and light
And I've held in my hands the stunned
Little bird til it turns and flies
Like my Lord holds me til I fly to Him
And eternity.
In earthly life
My loves, trust Him and me,
Come soon, and with joy.

* * *

A Letter from Michael Randall

October 5, 2010

Dear All,

Thank you Wendy for your email to all, I wanted to say something to you all but I could find no words. Thank you too Elizabeth for telephoning and I am sorry I could speak no words. Tonight I think will be the worst night, even more than her peaceful final departure on the 13th. I knew I had lost the love of my life in that terrible moment when I switched on the light and realised the awful reality and with no way to say goodbye. So I must live with the nightmare memories of this anniversary night and then move on. As I look at the photographs in front of me, I give thanks for her love and all of her she gave to you all to help make you into the wonderful people you are. I also give thanks that she is at peace having lived life to the full while devoting herself to us. We are fortunate people and I thank you all for your love and support over the past fleeting year. It would have been a desolate time without that. It must be every bit as bad for you; she had been there for all the formative years of your lives, so I must not wallow in my own sadness. I am OK really, it is just a bad time.

Jonathan came to see me this afternoon which was kind and thoughtful of him. He and Sandra have just got back from Canada. I hope everything goes well for your trip there tomorrow, Wendy and Johnnie.

I can't focus to read this so I hope it makes some sort of sense.

Much love,

Daddy

* * *

Figure 127. Daphne and Michael at Catherine and Grayson's Wedding, Oxford, 10 September 1988

Appendix IV
Miscellaneous Photos

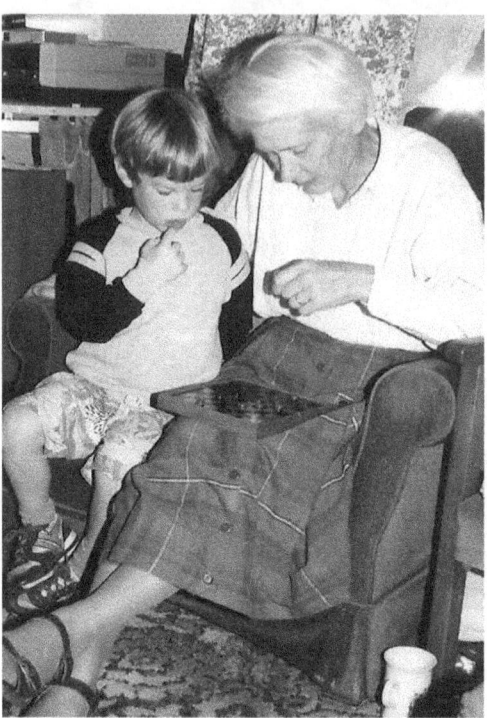

Figure 128. Daphne with Michael Griffiths, Westbury, Wiltshire, c. 1990

Figure 129. Daphne and Elizabeth, with Katie Carter, Westbury, Wiltshire, c.1991

Appendix IV ~ Miscellaneous Photos 171

Figure 130. Daphne with Katie Carter, c.1991, Westbury, Wiltshire,

Figure 131. Daphne and Michael Randall, Westbury, Wiltshire, c.2004;

Figure 132. Daphne on the Mower, Westbury, Wiltshire, c.2004

Figure 133. Wendy and Johnnie's Wedding, St. James' Church, Staveley, Cumbria, c.2004, with the parents and all eight siblings in attendance.

Appendix IV ~ Miscellaneous Photos 173

Figure 134. Daphne Serving Lunch, Westbury, Wiltshire, c.2004

*Figure 135. Michael, Abigail Carter, Daphne and Catherine Carter
Rear Garden, Westbury, Wiltshire, c. 2007*

Figure 136
Family Photograph, Fiftieth Anniversary Celebration of the Wedding of Michael and Daphne Randall, July 2006, in the Garden at Westbury, Wiltshire. (l-r) John, Elizabeth, Charles, Catherine, Wendy, Annie, Daphne, Michael, Rosemary, and Muriel

Appendix V

Family Tree:
Daphne Muriel Kelly

Appendix V ~ Family Tree

Daphne Muriel Kelly Family Tree

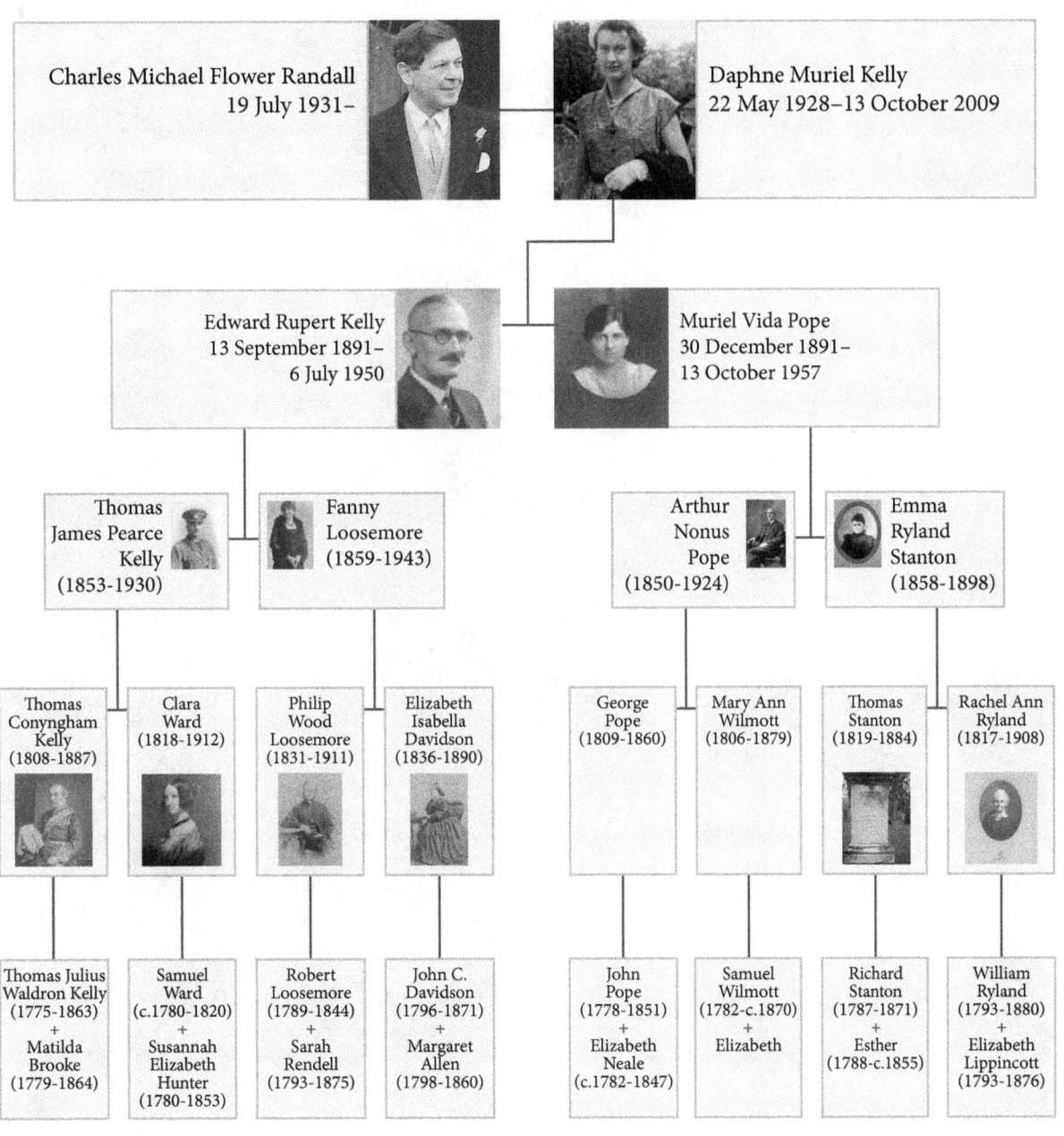